Stages

Frontispiece: Reynard the Fox at the court of King Noble, by
Wilhelm von Kaulbach, from Goethe's *Reineke Fuchs*, 1846.

In Praise of FLATTERY

WILLIS GOTH REGIER

University of Nebraska Press : Lincoln and London

Library of Congress
Cataloging-in-Publication Data
Regier, Willis Goth.
In praise of flattery / Willis Goth
Regier.
p.   cm. — (Stages)
Includes bibliographical
references and index.
ISBN-13: 978-0-8032-3969-2
(cloth: alk. paper)
1. Etiquette. 2. Flattery. 3. Praise.
I. Title.
BJ1838.R44   2007
177'.3 — dc22   2007007625

Set in Minion Pro by Bob Reitz.
Designed by A. Shahan.

For parents, grandparents, and godparents

And for Anna Louise and Marie Eileen Kinderman

The whole World and the Bus'ness of it,
is Manag'd by Flattery and Paradox;
the one sets up False Gods,
and the other maintains them.

SIR ROGER L'ESTRANGE, *Fables*

CONTENTS

ILLUSTRATIONS

Preface

Goethe admitted, "So true it is that whatever inwardly confirms man in his self-conceit, or flatters his secret vanity, is so highly desirable to him, that he does not ask further, whether in other respects it may turn to his honor or disgrace."[1] That's where flattery leads: to honor or disgrace.

This book is a shortcut, whatever way you're headed. If you're in a hurry, it will reduce bumps and detours. If you have time to kill, these pages will pardon it. For company you'll have lusty royalty, learned saints, and military geniuses. The argument capers like a hound, runs off, and returns with something for you between its teeth.

Set your pace to a stroll. Stop whenever you want. Interrupt, jump back and forth, I won't mind. This book should be as easy as laughter. It is stuffed with small things to take away. Please help yourself.

Flattery has warm and fuzzy anecdotes, fashions and traditions, old tricks and new ones. It is sweet, sticky, addictive, and as full of surprises as a new lover. It gets its kicks by flirting with insult and ridicule. You'll see.

New for the millennium, Richard Stengel's *(You're Too Kind): A Brief History of Flattery* (2000) gave flattery studies a fresh start and a family tree by beginning with chimpanzees, who flatter each other for sex, status, and survival. "The word that primatologists use over and over to describe chimpanzee behavior is 'Machiavellian.'"[2] (Machiavelli and flattery mix like vermicelli and pesto.) I am grateful that Stengel treated higher primates—Capellanus, Castiglione, Lord Chesterfield, Tocqueville, and Dale Carnegie—saving me the trouble. Though the topic requires that I cross his path now and then, I explore different places. We agree that flattery is inevitable, deceptively trivial, and sometimes inspired.

Royal courts are flattery's most famous laboratories. Its masters include Cleopatra, Shakespeare, and Disraeli, its color is purple, its domain reaches round the globe. "O power of flattery! How far you extend, and how wide are the frontiers of your pleasant realm!" exclaimed Cervantes.[3]

Fighting my fondness for poetry and fiction (not always successfully), I thought it preferable to pick examples of real flattery in real situations. Hundreds of such examples follow; there could have been hundreds more, but many are too much alike. One historian to another, David Hume advised Edward Gibbon, "Men run with great avidity to give their evidence in favor of what flatters their passions and their national prejudices."[4]

I rely heavily on multivolume histories, political tracts, and memoirs of kings, queens, and their circles. I have been partial to authors who held high office, historians like Tacitus, Burke, and Guizot, and statesmen like Franklin and Cicero. Sacred texts and members of the clergy are cited. Shamefully, for thousands of years, flattery by women has been admonished rather than recorded, with scarce exceptions. Athenaeus mentions the *Kolakides*, women who specialized in flattering powerful women, but says little about them.[5] I give you the rivalries of Versailles.

Flattery flourished in imperial China and classical Greece. Otto Ribbeck's *Kolax* (1883), the single most important book on flattery, focuses on Greek classics. The basic Greek corpus includes Aesop (sixth century BC), who stereotyped the flattering fox; Plato (circa 427–347 BC), who famously described a flatterer [παράσιτος] as "a fearsome and most pernicious creature"; and Plutarch (circa AD 45–120), whose "How to Tell a Flatterer from a Friend" is the core text of flattery studies.[6] Athenaeus (circa AD 170–circa 230) records the names, gains, and failures of famous flatterers of the ancient world: Tithymallus, Chairephon, Moschion.

Roman historians chronicled the infestation of the empire with flatterers. A fine phrase from Tacitus, "blanditiae sunt pessimum veri adfectus venenum" [flattery is the worst poison of true affection], became a literary commonplace.[7]

Flattery decorated the Italian Renaissance. Raphael flattered the papacy. Michelangelo flattered the Medici. Machiavelli flatters and gives flattery advice in *The Prince* (1513), a guide as useful for managing a prince as for being one.

Flattery abounded in the 1600s and 1700s. Louis XIV, La Fontaine, La Rochefoucauld, Saint-Simon, Gibbon, Burke, and Samuel Johnson returned to it again and again.

Not long ago there was a vogue for "secret memoirs," high-end scandal mongering, some of it possibly true. One example illustrates them all. In 1815 Charles Doris published his *Secret Memoirs of Napoleon Buonaparte*, claiming to reveal the emperor's private life in the last fifteen years of his glory. Doris set himself

> a plan, the most inconceivable, the most difficult, perhaps the most dangerous that could ever have entered into the ideas of man. This was to pursue a constant and unvaried study of the character of Buonaparte, physically, as well as morally; to observe him alike in public and in private, by day and by night, in a word at every moment when I could approach him, could hear him. I saw him daily, but not constantly; on occasions of very particular interest I quitted him, except when he was in his fits of passion—I was then his master. The sort of carelessness and semi-idiotism which I outwardly assumed when with him, placed me above the reach of suspicion, and delivered him up to me entirely.

And what did this semi-idiotic master of Napoleon see? "A disgusting assemblage of meanness, of imposture, of self-interest, of servile adulation, or corruption, of incapacity!—It seemed a contest who should degrade themselves most before the idol. Every thing in Buonaparte was false, but a part of his court was still more so;—if he ruled France with a rod of iron, it was forged by his flatterers. From the days of Pharamond to his days, never was a monarch flattered so incessantly, so servilely."[8] Doris begins with superlative self-flattery ("most inconceivable, most difficult, most dangerous") and ends by condemning flatterers. This is typical. The history of flattery is crossed with contradictions, blurred by codes, spread by spies, and double-crossed by hypocrisy, that most tenacious of confusions.

Thinkers who think about flattery, flatterers avid to apply it, and potentates raised or ruined by it repeat a set of standard lessons, here collected. You don't have to wear a powdered wig or risk a duel to learn the lessons they learned. They strained and suffered; you need only read about them. Because flattery is fleeting, you needn't read much.

This book about flattery is short because flattery should be quick and to the point. For easy use, the rules of flattery are numbered and printed conspicuously. I take the format from Balzac's *Physiology of Marriage* (1829). You can learn a lot about flattery from Balzac, but his books are longer, older, fiction, and French.[9]

Now, onward! To honor or disgrace!

1. Welcome

> When Fortune flatters,
> she comes to ensnare.
>
> **PUBLILIUS SYRUS**

When is praise praiseworthy and when not?

Tyrants want praise so much they demand it by the stadiumful, but forced praise is near screams and weeping. Voluntary praise is the kind most people value. It comes in three types.[1]

1. Spontaneous praise given to someone who has earned it. This type is precious and abundant: it happens on first dates, after home repair and school recitals, and during speeches and sports events.

2. Prepared praise given to someone who has earned it. Praises at graduations, retirements, and religious ceremonies are carefully rehearsed. Such praise can be as sublime as an orchestra and choir.

3. Praise, either spontaneous or prepared, given whether earned or not, in order to get something in return. This is flattery.[2]

↪ RULE 1: *When praise seeks a reward, it is flattery.*

"The two main Ends of Flattery are Profit or Safety," said Sir Roger L'Estrange, but not all flattery is scheming or venal: often flattery seeks nothing more than to be liked and noticed.[3] Not all flattery is selfish: parents flatter for their children's sake, and friends for friends'. Only the witless dismiss flattery as worthless. On the contrary, flattery has a price, and if it's very good, the price can be very high. William Hazlitt wrote, "Flattery and submission are marketable commodities like any other, have their price, and ought scarcely to be obtained under false pretences."[4]

The great Greek sage Plutarch goes to the heart of the matter: "The flatterer allures by means of pleasures and concerns himself with pleasures."[5]

✤ RULE 2: *Praise must please.*

If it does not please, it's noise. Excellent flattery can be so pleasing that it can be perceived as flat-out flattery and please even so. Excellent flatterers welcome attentive audiences; mighty potentates enjoy public praise. In the most pleasing situation, a flatterer would genuinely admire the flatteree, please that person, please other present company, be pleased to stagger rivals, and get something out of it: applause, promotion, a favor, reciprocal praise. Flattery is as social as a banquet.

✤ RULE 3: *Flattery civilizes.*

Bernard Mandeville thought flattery took the first step toward civilization. Primitive people

> thoroughly examin'd all the Strength and Frailties of our Nature, and observing that none were either so savage as not to be charm'd with Praise, or so despicable as patiently to bear Contempt, justly concluded, that Flattery must be the most powerful Argument that could be used to Human Creatures. Making use of this bewitching Engine, they extoll'd the Excellency of our Nature above other Animals, and setting forth with unbounded Praises the Wonders of our Sagacity and Vastness of Understanding, bestow'd a thousand Encomiums on the Rationality of our Souls, by the Help of which we were capable of performing the most noble Atchievements.[6]

Flattery is an advanced form of animal mimicry. Edmund Burke, counselor of parliaments and kings, observed that "it is by imitation far more than by precept, that we learn everything; and what we learn thus, we acquire not only more effectually, but more pleasantly. This forms our manners, our opinions, our lives. It is one of the strongest links of society; it is a species of mutual compliance, which all men yield to each other, without constraint to themselves, and which is extremely flattering to all."[7]

↜ RULE 4: *Anything praise can do, flattery can imitate.*

Imitation creates a community—people dress alike, sound alike, share similar views—and makes sharp distinctions of small differences. Madame de Maintenon, beloved of Louis XIV, advised her circle to imitate "with ingenuity."[8] Like everything else in society, imitation has limits, and flattery has boundaries beyond which lie censure and ridicule.

↜ RULE 5: *To stand out, flattery must fit in.*

When flattery is misplaced it is fatal to a flatterer. A flatterer must be able to work a crowd or flatter a target in the midst of one. The audience needs to be taken into account, not just the person flattered, and not only the present audience but possible future ones. "Holbein, according to legend, so flattered Anne of Cleves that Henry VIII mar-

1. Hans Holbein's portrait of Anne of Cleves (circa 1539) did not show her smallpox scars. On the basis of the portrait, Henry VIII drew up a marriage contract. The king had a different impression upon seeing Anne herself; he divorced her six months later.

ried her on the strength of the likeness, with the result that as soon as the King saw the original the painter had to fly the country."[9]

The well-known line "Imitation is the sincerest of flattery" comes from the Reverend Charles Caleb Colton's *Lacon* (1820).[10] His book sold well, thanks in large part to his energy in promoting it. Colton sailed away from money trouble in Britain to publish the work in the United States, where it was quickly taken up and often reprinted.[11]

On the title page of *Lacon* Colton addresses his book "*to those who think*," brash immediate flattery. Colton admits it is a marketing tactic: "Although the proportion of those who *do* think be extremely small, yet every individual flatters himself that he is *one* of the number."[12] How does Rev. Colton think? Shrewdly. One of his publishers described him as a pious fraud, an eloquent beggar, a cheat: "a man of low, groveling, and vicious propensities." Colton was also author of "Hypocrisy: A Satirical Poem." His parishioners believed it was a subject he knew well.[13]

Rev. Colton found flattery at church, inn, and polling place. He observed a firm rule:

↬ RULE 6: *Insults can flatter.*

"Some who affect to dislike flattery, may yet be flattered indirectly, by a well seasoned abuse and ridicule of their rivals. Diogenes professed to be no flatterer; but his cynic raillery was, in other words, flattery; it fed the ruling passion of the Athenian mob, who were more pleased to hear their superiors abused, than themselves commended."[14] Oliver Wendell Holmes wrote of "the perpetual *flattery of abuse*" suffered by reformers.[15]

Abuse is flattery's heritage. Aristotle thought that "to be a flatterer is a reproach."[16] Rather, to be known as nothing *but* a flatterer is a reproach. As if vilification were a virtue, they who flatter badly hiss those who flatter well.

↬ RULE 7: *Flattery is always under attack.*

For centuries an absurdity was proverbial: "plus nocet lingua adulatoris quam manus persecutoris" [the tongue of the flatterer hurts more than the sword of the persecutor], hyperbolic humbug. Wherever flattery thrives it is denounced as "the handmaid of vice," "that filthy science," "the worst of vices," the "prostitution of empty praise," and the like.[17]

Biblical flattery is concentrated in the Old Testament — Jacob flattered Esau, hypocrites flattered God — and further concentrated in Proverbs, which warns, "A man who flatters his neighbor is spreading a net for his feet" (Proverbs 29:5). In his *Imitation of Christ*, Thomas à Kempis advised the Christian to avoid flatterers, strangers, women, the young, and the rich — or, failing that, to become a monk.[18] Despite recurring condemnations of it, Christianity took to flattery as it did to imperial Rome. Inspired Christians have produced much of the world's most memorable flattery.

↬ RULE 8: *Flattery thrives in religion.*

Priests, pastors, and pontiffs have railed against flattery and have been railed against for loving it. Nothing human is pure enough, not even religion, to repel pretensions, prevarications, and flattery. In 1771 Samuel Adams asked, "But are we not fallen into an age when *some* even of the Clergy think it no shame to *flatter the Idol*; and thereby to lay the people, as in the days of *Jeroboam, the son of Nebat*, under a temptation to commit great wickedness, and sin against God? Let us beware of the poison of flattery."[19] By "*Idol*" Adams meant King George; by citing Jeroboam he meant any king.

Bad flatterers make bad flattery, giving all flattery a bad name.[20] The eighteenth century was especially peeved about it. Samuel Johnson's *Dictionary* (1756) defines "cajole," "coax," "cog," "collogue," "daub," "fawn," "glose," "paw," and "smooth" as "flatter"; John Ash's *Dictionary* (2nd edition, 1795) adds "blandish," "claw," "court," "curry," "glaver," and "wheedle." Nowadays harsh words like "boot-licker," "kiss-ass," and " brownnose" label the worst sorts of flatterer, though, to be fair, to claw and glaver may be all a kiss-ass can do. Because bad flattery stinks and it's everywhere, little attention will be given to it here. This book will emphasize good flattery—indeed, the best. For the best, one rule reigns supreme:

↦ RULE 9: *Flattery works best when it's true.*

For a flatterer, lying is precarious. A flatterer with a bad reputation will be a bad flatterer. A flattering rival cannot be trusted, no matter what words sweetly spill. Writing of the Russian court of Catherine the Great, Charles Masson described as base and servile those who "know not how to be polite without meanness, or to flatter without falsehood."[21] At its best, flattery is truth well dressed, and it is best dressed with fine see-through fabrics. Honest flattery can caress a lover, cover up a gaffe, and muffle aggression.

A first-class flatterer delivers decent, respectable flattery that can be repeated without blushing. First-class flattery ripples awhile. All formal praises—toasts, odes, introductions, elegies, obituaries, letters of recommendation—are made better or worse by the freshness and flavor of their flattery.

↦ RULE 10: *The quality of flattery is judged by results.*

Originality is good, but not always necessary. Some flatteries have hardened into etiquette and some improve with repetition. You flatter your conversation partners when you agree with what they say; you delight them if you repeat their words as if they're matchless. Reliance on the already said is safe practice, but an ambitious flatterer needs to be able to create compliments on the spot. For this, certain habits are useful. Magnification is most obvious.

✦ RULE 11: *Flattery tends to exaggerate.*

Flattery is the zoom lens of psycho-optics. It hyperbolizes anything, especially when flattering oneself. Memoirs and autobiographies confirm the rule: Paramahansa Yogananda's *Autobiography of a Yogi* stretches incredibly. There have been momentous occasions when flattery claimed that men are gods, a topic so supercharged it serves as the climax to this book.

An artful flatterer instills a desire for more flattery and will not give too much. Amateurs hesitate, or worse, they gush. Napoleon's appetite for flattery pushed to the limit. "All the exaggerations of flattery were exhausted during the Consulate; and in the years which followed, it was necessary for poets often to repeat themselves. Thus, in the couplets of Lyons, the First Consul was the *God of victory, the conqueror of the Nile and of Neptune, the savior of his country, the peacemaker of the world, the arbiter of Europe.* The French soldiers were transformed into *friends and companions of Alcides,* etc., all of which was cutting the ground from under the feet of the singers of the future."[22]

✦ RULE 12: *Flattery is spoiled by excess.*

Much can be too much. Louis XIV told Racine, "I would praise you more if you had praised me less." Lucian of Samosata warned that intelligent potentates despise overdone praise. His example is Aristobulus who, to impress Alexander the Great, "inserted in his history an account of a single combat between Alexander and Porus [a king of India], and selected this passage to read aloud to the former; he reckoned that his best chance of pleasing was to invent heroic deeds for the king, and heighten his achievements." He reckoned wrong. Alexander angrily took the book, tossed it in the river, and threatened to toss Aristobulus after it.[23]

↜ RULE 13: *Flattery is a science.*[24]

Flattery needs to be carefully calibrated. It improves with education, it advances through close observation of cause and effect, and it is based on repeated experience. Among fine-tuned people, flattery requires almost atomic precision.

↜ RULE 14: *Flattery is an art.*

It seeks emotional response, it assumes personality (sometimes more than one), and it has masterpieces and grotesques.[25] Gibbon described flattery as "the most useful of all arts," an opinion he derived from a close study of the history of emperors.[26] "'Tis the finest of the Arts," George Meredith quipped. "We might call it moral sculpture. Adepts in it can cut their friends to any shape they like by practicing it with the requisite skill. I myself, poor hand as I am, have made a man act Solomon by constantly praising his wisdom."[27] Relying on nothing but the momentary pleasure of compliments, flattery works on more powerful emotions, or it doesn't work.

Machiavelli entitled the twenty-third chapter of *The Prince* "How to Avoid Flatterers" and gives sound, time-tested advice. He proposes this simile: "Just as those who paint landscapes place themselves in a low position on the plain in order to consider the nature of the mountains and the high places and place themselves atop mountains in order to study the plains, in like manner, to know well the nature of a people one must be a prince, and to know well the nature of princes one must be of the people."[28] Machiavelli warns against flatterers—all flatterers do—but first he flatters. How? By comparing the ideal prince to a painter in the hills.

↩ RULE 15: *Potentates like to be praised for their artistic sensitivity.*

Without them we would have poor architecture, less opera, no ballet, desolate galleries, and unperformed symphonies. The art of flattery enriches every other art.

A person who has every advantage to get ahead, except flattery, will sooner or later compete with someone else who has flattery, too. Intelligence, good looks, natural charm, and loyalty can be outmaneuvered by a charming intelligent flatterer.

↩ RULE 16: *In a man's world the best flatterers are women.*

Saint-Simon described the Princesse des Ursins, the perfect flatterer for the court of Louis XIV.

> She was rather tall than otherwise, a brunette, with blue eyes of the most varied expression, in figure perfect, with a most exquisite bosom; her face, without being beautiful, was charming; she was extremely noble in air, very majestic in demeanour, full of graces so natural and so continual in everything, that I have never seen any one approach her, either in form or mind. Her wit was copious and of all kinds: she was flattering, caressing, insinuating, moderate, wishing to please for pleasing's sake, with charms irresistible when she strove to persuade and win over; accompanying all this, she had a grandeur that encouraged instead of frightening; a delicious conversation, inexhaustible and very amusing, for she had seen many countries and persons; a voice and way of speaking extremely agreeable, and full of sweetness. She had read much, and reflected much. She knew how to choose the best society, how to receive them, and could even have held a court; was polite, distinguished; and above all was careful never to take a step in advance without dignity and discretion. She was eminently fitted for intrigue.[29]

Assisted by other skills (the more the better), aspiring flatterers climb to higher positions. In the daily realignment of the pecking order, they grab every advantage they can. Flattery is less potent than scandal or lies, less imposing than bribes or bodyguards, but it infiltrates every relationship to some degree.

Flattery fattens over dinner. The banquet conversation of Athenaeus's *Deipnosophists* evaluates flatterers as παράσιτοι [parasites], citing numerous ancient authorities. This, for instance, from Timocles: "If you grant that sociability is one of the virtues, your parasite practices that to perfection."[30] Aldous Huxley supposed, "It's flattering to have parasites. It's a compliment to the quality of your blood." Emerson believed that "huge animals nourish huge parasites, and the rancor of the disease attests the strength of the constitution." Nietzsche's Zarathustra proclaimed, "Whoever is of the highest species will nourish the most parasites." George Bernard Shaw agreed, "Man is the only animal which esteems itself rich in proportion to the number and voracity of its parasites."[31] A body without a flatterer is nobody in particular.

⊹ RULE 17: *The presence of flatterers is a sign of power.*

Some flatterees require better flatterers, as some palates demand better cooks. Colton saw that "we must suit the flattery to the mind and taste of the recipient. We do not put essences into hogsheads, or porter into vials."[32] If the best flatterers are found among mighty potentates, who should wonder? The rich and powerful are attractive. Some seek fame and enjoy it; some prefer privacy and a few close friends. All potentates are accustomed to flattery and many are skillful at it.

Cranks who condemn flattery as praise spoiled by ambition should shut up. Ambition and flattery go together perfectly, like electricity and wire.

↬ RULE 18: *Ambition is the fuel of flattery.*

What makeup was touched up, what book written, what sport practiced, without the ambition to be admired? Burke again:

> God has planted in man a sense of ambition, and a satisfaction
> arising from the contemplation of his excelling his fellows in
> something deemed valuable amongst them. It is this passion that
> drives men to all the ways we see in use of signalizing themselves,
> and that tends to make whatever excites in a man the idea of this
> distinction so very pleasant. It has been so strong as to make very
> miserable men take comfort, that they were supreme in misery;
> and certain it is that, where we cannot distinguish ourselves by
> something excellent, we begin to take a complacency in some sin-
> gular infirmities, follies, or defects of one kind or other. It is on
> this principle that flattery is so prevalent; for flattery is no more
> than what raises in a man's mind an idea of a preference which
> he has not.[33]

Like a cunning entrepreneur, flattery takes a little and makes a lot.
First-class flatterers master flattery's formulas and constantly inno-
vate. In the presence of power they flatter with loudspeakers.

Goebbels, Hitler's indefatigable flatterer, "took a particular interest
in radio and soon had complete control over it." He considered this
medium "the instrument par excellence — until such a time as televi-
sion should be developed — for influencing the masses." On April 20,
1933, Hitler's birthday, Goebbels broadcast a speech hailing Hitler
as "the savior of the nation," a phrase he would often repeat.[34]

↬ RULE 19: *Flattery exploits mass media.*

Reading a newspaper reporting on his remarks, Napoleon said to
Marshal Duroc, "It must be confessed, my dear Duroc, that courtiers are a class of men highly favored by heaven. They see twice as

much as other people; they even hear what has never been said; for I own to you, they attribute to me the finest speeches, of which I have never uttered a single word."

"Since it is for the glory of the state," said Duroc, "let them have their full range."[35]

Flattery among friends is mutually sustaining; for society everywhere flattery is a fact of life. Job seekers and recruiters butter and fudge with flattery. Teachers and tutors flatter to encourage. Lawyers flatter juries. "Excellent choice," says the waiter, no matter what you choose. "This flatters your figure," says the shopgirl to the stooge. Why flatter? "Excellent question," says the public speaker.

2. Flatter Yourself

> Everybody is himself
> his own foremost
> and greatest flatterer,
> and hence finds no
> difficulty in admitting
> the outsider to
> witness with him and
> to confirm his own
> conceits and desires.
>
> PLUTARCH

"I flatter myself" was a phrase in favor among American revolutionaries. George Washington, James Madison, and Alexander Hamilton used the phrase publicly. Benjamin Franklin flattered himself in his *Autobiography* by quoting flattering things said about him, "still more pleasing, as being so many spontaneous Testimonies of the public's good Opinion, and by me entirely unsolicited."[1] If these great souls could flatter themselves, why not you?

This book's high goal is to help you flatter yourself. The more you flatter yourself, the more useful it will be. It puts you in the midst of mighty potentates. It begins and ends with you. Sir Francis Bacon, patron of science, wrote, "There is no such flatterer as is a man's self," to say nothing about women.[2] For your sake and mine, you are hereby invited to view flattery's disarming array.

Who do you dream yourself to be? What boosts your pride? Why do you love yourself? How? How do you justify the pain you inflict and endure? Your dreams, love, pride, judgments, and pain bound your exposure to flattery. If you are smart, ambitious, and have an open heart you have an immense frontier. Of course you are smart, or you wouldn't be reading a book. How smart? Look to your flatteries. Like resolute pioneers, flatteries stretch the limits, little by little, way out there. Keep an eye on your susceptibility to flattery; it is a kind of skin, and it gives you the best hints you'll ever get about the susceptibilities of others.

Sages and oracles say that first wisdom is to *know thyself*. The more you know about how and why you flatter thyself, the better you'll be able to flatter others, and to appreciate how they flatter thee. If you flatter yourself properly you will be better able to enjoy yourself. Stretch your joy so that others enjoy you too. If you are your own worst enemy, make friends.

↦ RULE 20: *Hard questions flatter.*

Here are a few: How much do you bother about how smart you are? How much do you fret about your body and face? Your voice? Your family? Pride paints a bull's-eye on the parts of you you most care about. Your decisions about how you divide yourself between other people, your ideas about how much you should work and play, can change abruptly, but come what may, you have a You whom you steadfastly wonder about. Your opinion of You is what you have to hold on to, to live up to, to answer to alone at night. Flattery flies to this You like a bee to a buttercup.

As pride loves praise and trophies, people will tell you promptly what flatteries they want. Lord Chesterfield advised his son, "Every man talks most of what he has most a mind to be thought to excel in. Touch him but there, and you touch him to the quick."[3]

↦ RULE 21: *Flattery probes strength.*

People perform for flattery and let you know when they think it's due. Told off a bozo? Bravo! New haircut? Beautiful! Fixed the light? What a difference! Flatter judges for their judgment, flatter workers for their work.[4]

Be completely honest with yourself: Do you flatter yourself well or badly? Do you flatter your power and kindness? Do you flatter yourself despite yourself? You have to ask. Otherwise you and yourself could make fools of each other, day after day. True, a little foolishness can be harmless and endearing, but when grief or regrets clog your throat and heart, when distress or dilemmas tear like hooks, when you feel too low for help to hear you, then you need the flatteries you tell yourself. A little flattery, like a warm bath and soft towel, will let you get along with yourself, lie down with yourself, and sleep.

After that, flattery helps waking and getting up. If no one else will flatter you to make something of yourself, flatter yourself. Self-flattery is always available: it can be your first resort or your last. Care for yourself enough to listen carefully to what you say to yourself.

⊹ RULE 22: *The most seductive flattery flatters the You you wish to be.*

What else is encouragement? Plutarch observed that "flatterers declare of the rich man that he is at the same time an orator and a poet, and, if he will, a painter and a musician." Stengel cites Lord Chesterfield citing Cardinal Richelieu, "undoubtedly the ablest statesman of his time, or perhaps of any other" who wished to be thought the best poet, too. Those who flattered him most successfully bypassed his excellence in politics and praised his poetry. "Why? Because he was sure of one excellency, and distrustful as to the other."[5] Flattery fills a need (see Rule 15), even an absurd one.

Like pollen on a honeybee, flattery clings to the things you tell yourself. In triumph and celebration self-flattery will set the level by which you measure other people's praise. You will instantly notice anyone who flatters you better than you do.

⊹ RULE 23: *No matter how well you flatter yourself, you can do better.*

Find your potential and flatter it. You owe it to your body to worry when flattery makes excuses. Flattery disables when it alibis. A self-respecting self-flattering soul won't stray far into fantasy. Flatter yourself critically. The same old self-flattery becomes a hypnotizing wheel; take it up like a buzz saw (watch your fingers), cut your habits like lumber, build a whole new You.[6] When self-flattery is turned up high it gets your adrenaline pumping, it rivets your attention.

If you despise self-flattery, perhaps you have not given it its due. Its dues are entirely up to you. Ask for more and you'll get more. Lord Halifax advises, "A Man must not so entirely fall out with Vanity, as not to take its Assistance in the doing great Things." La Rochefoucauld noticed, "Virtue would not go nearly so far if vanity did not keep her company."[7]

If you rank self-criticism above self-flattery, perhaps you're too hard on yourself. Perhaps you think that you think about yourself too much and would rather think of anything else, a cause, a cosmos, a game. Then you're looking at yourself in the wrong places and could use a little nudge to get to your sensible parts. This book is a patient guide, ever ready to help you get there, wherever you start, whenever you want, step-by-step, by spurts, or skipping.

Flatterers congregate around potentates, but you needn't fret if you cannot flatter a monarch. There is someone much closer and more important. Who? Oh, you know. You. Flattery examines one You after another, in search of whatever good can come from any.

❧ RULE 24: *Insert your own rule here.*

Unless you grew up on the moon you first learned about flattery as a child. You've been picking up bits and pieces ever since. You do not need to be a philosopher to think a lot about yourself, but like Aristotle brooding over ethics, if you're seriously thinking about what you think of yourself you will sooner or later wonder what good it does you. Talks with yourself should yield more than a reliable echo or sincere self-pity. You need to be persuaded that you are worth talking to, that you and yourself can get past grudges, guilt, and other barricades.

Can you lie to yourself and get away with it? Take it from an expert: you can.

The expert is François VI, duc de La Rochefoucauld (1613–80), peer of France, prince of Marcillac, baron of Vérteuil, Montignac, and Cahuzac, and retainer to His Majesty Louis XIV.[8] Three times wounded and nearly blinded in the French civil wars, entrusted with great duties and imprisoned in the Bastille, partisan and victim of court intrigues, champion of the queen and by the queen betrayed,

La Rochefoucauld observed hypocrisy on a grand scale. Ecclesiastes is the primer on vanity; La Rochefoucauld's *Maxims* (1664) is for upper classes. This rule is found on its first page:

✎ RULE 25: *"Self-love is the greatest of all flatterers."*[9]

In the first edition of *Maxims* La Rochefoucauld included a short essay on *amour-propre* [self-love], confident that he describes every self, not just his own. "It would thus seem that the desires of self-love are kindled, not by the glow or worth of what attracts it, but by its own efforts; that its own cravings create value and add embellishment; that what it pursues is itself, and that it is pleasing itself in seeking the things it finds pleasant. It is a mass of opposites: imperious and submissive, sincere and deceitful, compassionate and cruel, timid and bold."[10] Does that resonate?

Speaking for his species, La Rochefoucauld declared, "We should have almost no pleasure if we never flattered ourselves."[11] He was a warrior caught at the court of King Louis, where libertines pecked at each other's etiquette. He saw self-love seething beneath silk and lace, flattery mingled with slander and bribes.

Speaking for the French nobility, he concluded: "We dislike to bestow praise, and we never do it without a selfish motive. Praise is a clever, delicate and masked form of flattery which differently satisfies the recipient and the donor: the one accepts it as a reward of merit, the other bestows it to prove how fair-minded he is, and how discerning."[12] Cynicism this smooth looks primped before a mirror.

Self-flattery cannot avoid itself; it might as well take a long hard look at itself. La Rochefoucauld's maxims are shamelessly self-referential, frank and confessional, and flatter the reader by bravely telling the truth. Truth, too, has pleasures. "Perspicacity has an air of clairvoyance which flatters our vanity more than all other qualities of mind."[13] To watch self-flattery at work, look closely. If you don't know how to look for it, it will blend in with the real and true, and seem real and true.

To surpass great monarchs in a few minutes, do no more than this: write down how you flatter yourself. Histories and memoirs report that royalty was perpetually flattered, but they rarely quote the flatteries. No need to save what is quickly replenished.

↭ RULE 26: *Most flattery does its work and disappears.*

There are flatteries in granite and marble, but most are as evanescent as kisses.[14] Flattery does not need to be brilliant or memorable — it can fall apart if analyzed — and it is sometimes most effective when whispered. The few occasions when ostentatious flattery is heartily expected — weddings, victories, funerals — are heavily formalized.

Does flattery work? Every chance it gets.

↭ RULE 27: *Flattery adapts to all emotions.*

Percy Shelley wrote that pity, admiration, and sympathy are "flattering emotions."[15] There are more. If you doubt yourself you flatter your intelligence. If you blame yourself you flatter your conscience. Love flatters lovers, fear flatters bullies. Apologies flatter. Twilights flatter. Flowers flatter. Oils and alcohol flatter. Words flatter better than anything else, except, on occasion, rapt silence (Rule 66). Letters, news reports, and scholarship flatter. History, law, and politics flatter. The whole apparatus of tradition and memorialization reveals "an impulse to remember what is attractive or flattering and to ignore all the rest."[16]

Are you ambitious to be all you can be? Then learn flattery, a reliable ladder. On his way toward becoming master of France, Richelieu "ingratiated himself to the Queen-Mother by a speech full of the most outrageous flattery." Talleyrand saw that with "a few flatteries, judiciously applied," Monsieur de Stainville became ambassador to Rome.[17]

⊹ RULE 28: *History begins with flattery.*

Plutarch and Tacitus complained that much so-called history was composed in order to flatter, and that it was difficult to sift the truth. Plutarch pined, "To such degree, it seems, is truth hedged about with difficulty and hard to capture by research, since those who come after the events in question find that lapse of time is an obstacle to their proper perception of them; while the research of their contemporaries into men's deeds and lives, partly through envious hatred and partly through fawning flattery, defiles and distorts the truth."[18]

⊹ RULE 29: *Literature begins with flattery.*

The oldest literatures of China, Egypt, and Greece commemorate conquerors. The oldest literature of India praises invincible chariots and cities set aflame. For epic flattery, there are epics. Flatterers immerse in sewage forever in the eighth circle of Dante's *Inferno*. Satan will not bow to man but flatters Eve in *Paradise Lost*. Rev. George Crabbe's mini-epic, "The Birth of Flattery," awards Flattery's paternity to Poverty and her maternity to Cunning. Flattery is, he says, the "Meed and Muse" of poets (Rule 56).[19]

The flatterer is a stock comic character the world over. In his *Eunuch* Terence presented Gnatho, the stereotypical flatterer, who trained himself to agree with anything. The second of Theophrastus's *Characters* is "The Flatterer." Menander produced a *Flatterer* for ancient Greece, Plautus produced one for republican Rome, and Charles Macklin's Sir Pertinax MacSycophant entertained London in the reign of George III. Literature teaches flattery faster than experience, and at less cost.

Animal fables feature flatterers. In the very first tale of Purnabhadra's *Panchatantra*, Damanaka the jackal says that he learned "the whole duty of a functionary" from the *Mahābhārata* and summarizes:

No burden enervates the strong;
To enterprise no road is long;
The well-informed all countries range;
    To flatterers no man is strange.[20]

The animal fables of Aesop, Babrius, Phaedrus, Marie de France, Gay, Lessing, Northcote, Florian, and La Fontaine feature flattering foxes, and Reynard the Fox (alias Reynke de Vos, Reinecke Fuchs, etc.) has been a popular antihero since (at least) the tenth century. Animal courtiers of the Lion King were warned, "Have great regard to your selfe, for Reynard is full of policy and knoweth how to dissemble, flatter and betray; he hath a world of snares to intangle you withall, and without great exercise of judgement, will make a scorne and mocke of the best wisdome breathing."[21] Goethe enlarged Reynard's fame in a verse retelling, often translated. The ablest of courtiers, Reynard prefers to stay at home, away from court, a dangerous place where rivals gang.

❧ RULE 30: *Flatterers flock.*

Flatterers make effective teams; loving couples and circles of friends mutually assist by flattering each other at parties and meetings. Madame de Montespan placed her siblings in strategic positions in the salons of Versailles. Throughout his *Maxims*, La Rochefoucauld chose plural first-person pronouns, as in Maxim 152, "If we did not flatter ourselves, the flattery of others would do us no harm," and 192, "When our vices desert us, we flatter ourselves that we are deserting our vices."[22] His "We" is truly a "We" and not just a leap to a higher level of generalization, though it is that, too. The *Maxims* began as a game played at the salon of Madame de Sablé, a game of maxims in which participants entertained each other by exchanging aphorisms and criticizing them. The first phase of composition was "more or less a collaboration" between La Rochefoucauld, Madame

2. "Reynard the Fox at the Court of the Lion King Nobel," by Walter Crane (1897), a scene often depicted in versions of *Reynard*.

de Sablé, and Jacques Esprit.[23] La Rochefoucauld's investigations into self-love were assisted by the love of others.

  ✤ RULE 31: *Flattery seeks mutuality.*

Souls in need of regular flattery form parties and join clubs. Hippolyte Taine described a club member: "The public, in his eyes, seems two hundred persons; their opinion weighs on him without any counterpoise, and, outside of their belief, which is his also, every other belief is absurd and even culpable. Moreover, he discovers through this constant system of preaching, which is nothing but flattery, that he is patriotic, intelligent, virtuous, of which he can have no doubt, because, before being admitted into the club, his civic virtues have been verified."[24] This smells of jealousy and is anyway unjust: a herd of mutual flatterers is more likely to survive and do more good than a flatterer alone on the prowl. Let us repeat La Rochefoucauld: "Virtue would not go nearly so far if vanity did not keep her company."

Flattering friends abate the need for self-flattery, and ought to reduce it. If self-flattery is not kept to yourself its tender skin pops like a balloon.

  ✤ RULE 32: *Self-flattery becomes conceit when it airs in public.*

Cicero spoiled his praises for others and blemished his own reputation forever by publicly praising himself. Better by far to exchange flatteries with loving friends and develop each other's tastes and repertoires.

On the grim side, flattery isn't what it used to be (Rule 94). Humans everywhere have had a high time celebrating species superiority. Only humans have fire, antennae in stellar space, enriched uranium, paychecks, and holidays. Superior as we are, we are so dense that even our brightest ideas take centuries to sink in. Billions despise the mob. Millions still root for the Master Race. Some proud humans, persuaded at last that their habits waste, pollute, and exterminate, postpone reform to flatter themselves for finding new ways to conquer nature.

On the bright side, flattery's proud past is recoverable, and its rusty old rules still operate. Some pious highly flattered nitwit will arise now and then to kick and flail at flattery, going on and on, and expecting praise for it. You could hear it a thousand times and what good would it do you? Better by far to know how flattery seeps and insinuates, better to defend yourself from it, better to recognize flattery addicts and their withdrawal symptoms. Better to flatter yourself frankly than succumb to sweet deceit.

Flattery, the art of appeal, is too precious a heritage to be lost without a fight, and it should not fight stupidly. By restoring flattery to its place in court, boardroom, bedroom, and meeting hall, this little book seeks to divert a few wise readers from narrow interests and shortsighted gain. La Rochefoucauld believed, "It is exceedingly silly to wish to be wise all alone."[25]

So back to you, as often as you like.

3. Why Flatter?

> In this disorganized society, in which the passions of the people are the sole real force, authority belongs to the party that understands how to flatter.

HIPPOLYTE TAINE

Why flatter? To soothe, ally, encourage, arouse, ameliorate, ingratiate, inspire, pacify, play, and always to please. In a world where power is all, flattery is a professional instrument, to be plied with other devices of confidence and intrigue. "A Fool that will Swallow Flattery, shall never want a Knave to give it him," Sir Roger L'Estrange wrote in 1692. "There is nothing which the majority of the world is more fond of than flattery," added George Wright in 1797. Forty years later Balzac cooed, "This two-footed soul will always accept as true those things which flatter his passions, caress his hates, or serve his amours: from this comes logic."[1]

Erasmus, wisest of humanists, defended flattery at length, giving its sunniest rationale:

There *is* a kind of flattery which is wholly noxious, and a good many treacherous persons use it in mockery in order to destroy their unfortunate victims. But the form I use stems from a sort of ingenuous goodness of heart and is far nearer being a virtue than the critical asperity which is its opposite: what Horace calls a harsh and disagreeable surliness. Mine raises downcast spirits, comforts the sad, rouses the apathetic, stirs up the stolid, cheers the sick, restrains the headstrong, brings lovers together and keeps them united. It attracts children to pursue the study of letters, makes old men happy, and offers advice and counsel to princes in the form of praise which doesn't give offence. In short, it makes everyone more agreeable and likeable to himself, and this is the main ingredient in happiness. . . . For the moment I'll say nothing about the large part flattery plays in your celebrated eloquence, a larger one in medicine and its largest in poetry, but will sum up by saying that it is what sweetens and gives savor to every human relationship.[2]

Why flatter? For sweetness and savor! A person well practiced in flattery is better able to praise.

↦ RULE 33: *Flattery is the school for praise.*

It is a painful embarrassment to be introduced to a Great Person, yet be tongue-tied for fear of uttering some stale compliment that the Great Person has heard a thousand times. Lonesome Nietzsche lamented flattery's modern destitution. "No one today understands how to pay homage or flatter with wit; this leads to the ludicrous fact that in cases where one *must* do homage (to a great statesman or artist, for example), one borrows the language of deepest feeling, of loyal and honorable decency—out of embarrassment and a lack of wit and grace. So men's public, ceremonious encounters seem ever more clumsy, but more tender and honorable, without being so."[3] A competent flatterer compliments fearlessly.

Flattery is indispensable for civil service. Stengel cites Henry Kissinger's "relentless and unctuous toadying to Richard Nixon."[4] Kissinger explained, "Nixon's favor depended on the readiness to fall in with the paranoid cult of the tough guy. The conspiracy of the press, the hostility of the Establishment, the flatulence of the Georgetown set, were permanent features of Nixon's conversations." When Nixon made some outrageous statement, Kissinger would say, "Yes, Mr. President, your analysis is absolutely correct and certainly very profound."[5]

Successful diplomats are flattery experts. Macaulay described the duties of an ambassador:

> Instead of consulting, by a reserved manner and ambiguous style, the dignity of those whom he represented, he was to plunge into all the intrigues of the Court at which he resided, to discover and flatter every weakness of the prince, and of the favorite who governed the prince, and of the lacquey who governed the favorite.

He was to compliment the mistress and bribe the confessor, to panegyrise or supplicate, to laugh or weep, to accommodate himself to every caprice, to lull every suspicion, to treasure every hint, to be everything, to observe everything, to endure everything.[6]

Because flattery can be abused, all flattery is suspicious, but that is not flattery's fault. It is a skill, a tool, no more nor less than speech is a tool; it can build or break.[7] For safety's sake its dangers are safely quarantined in chapter 6; by the time you get there you'll be inoculated. But first things first, and first, what good can flattery do?

Flattery belongs at first encounters. Introductions are ideal occasions for it. "How good to meet you! I've heard so much about you." Kind, thoughtful flattery speeds acquaintance to friendship and preferment.

↪ RULE 34: *Flattery makes friends.*

The novelty of a new friendship is brightened by the interest taken in knowing all the goodness of the friend. Flattery coaxes goodness to come forth so that dialogue and information flow. In a gush of proverbs Shakespeare made plain: "There is flattery in friendship."[8]

↪ RULE 35: *Careful flattery expresses care.*

Plutarch recognized that flattery, "which blends itself with every emotion, every moment, need, and habit, is hard to separate from friendship." In his series of encouraging letters to Coleridge, Charles Lamb called him "a man who writes blank verse like Milton. Now, this is delicate flattery, *indirect* flattery."[9] Lamb flatters himself to think this delicate, and the italics of *indirect* direct the eye to his emphasis. Tolstoy, too, wrote about the "delicate flattery" common in friendship, "that delicate flattery that goes hand in hand with conceit, and consists in a tacit assumption that one's companion and oneself are the only people capable of understanding all the folly of the rest of the world and the sagacity and profundity of their own ideas."[10] Tolstoy is too harsh: intimate friends can enjoy their sense of superiority, even congratulate themselves for it, for the very good reason that their intimacy exists. Whole nations pride themselves because they are nations.

↬ RULE 36: *Flatteries learned in friendship can turn enemies into friends.*

Insults start wars; flatteries prefer peace (gruesome exceptions will be noted). The masterful general Alcibiades was adept at disarming others. "No disposition could resist and no nature escape Alcibiades, so full of grace was his daily life and conversation. Even those who feared and hated him felt a rare and winning charm in his society and presence. And thus it was that Tissaphernes, though otherwise the most ardent of the Persians in his hatred of the Hellenes, so completely surrendered to the flatteries of Alcibiades as to outdo him in reciprocal flatteries." Similarly, Senator Martius Verus exerted "a quality of charm about all that he said or did, a charm that soothed the vexation and anger of everyone while raising their hopes even more. He knew the proper time for flattery and presents and entertainment at table. . . . he made it plain to the barbarians that his friendship was more worth striving for than his enmity."[11]

The high correlation between tyrants and flatterers led penny moralists to treat them like vermin from the same swamp. This is unjust to flatterers. Tyrannical personalities ill disposed to contradiction can explode instantly and endanger innocent bystanders. Insulating layers of flatterers muffle the blow.

↬ RULE 37: *Flattery encourages improvement.*

In the daily routines of ordinary life, flattery inspires and encourages. La Rochefoucauld concluded, "The desire to be worthy of the praise we receive strengthens our powers of virtue; and the praise bestowed on our wit, our courage and our appearance helps to enhance them."[12]

Where do wit, courage, and appearance need more encouragement than in courtship?

↬ RULE 38: *Flattery sweetens love.*

I balk to state such an obvious truth but cannot omit it: budding and lasting loves uphold flattery as well as any other advocate. "You are the best" (or more timidly, "You are the best for me"), "You fulfill me," "You make life worth living," and the like are the glues that seal love's compact. If no one understood English better than Shakespeare, no one knew flattery better. He invited it: "O, flatter me; for love delights in praises."[13] Lovers and flatterers seek to please. When urged to flatter by a lover's wish, a lover will please still more if the flattery is impromptu and free of cliché. Loving flattery taps all the resources of self-expression.

↬ RULE 39: *Flattery encourages virtue.*

It can also encourage vice, but give virtue its due. Flattery encourages work. Pliny knew that his publishers were flattering him, and took it well. "Well, let them flatter, as long as their lies make me pursue my studies." Tolstoy idealized a hostess capable of a "subtle, unostentatious, peculiar flattery" that made a guest "once again aware of his virtues and afforded him a pleasurable sense of satisfaction." Robert Smith Surtees sums up, "More people are flattered into virtue than bullied out of vice."[14]

↪ RULE 40: *Flattery encourages competition.*

The power of praise to encourage and inspire has long been understood by military leaders. The *Arthashastra* of Kautilya (second century AD) advised the rajas of India to prepare their armies for battle with bards and praise singers. "They shall extol the clan, group, family, deeds and conduct of the warriors."[15]

↪ RULE 41: *Flattery assuages defeat.*

When wars go badly flattery soothes. After the Romans suffered serious losses in Germany, Tiberius sought "the antidote" in sycophancy, and raised statues of himself with religious ceremony.[16]

Why flatter? To appease ruthless potentates who demand flattery and to defend yourself against ruthless flatterers.

↪ RULE 42: *Familiarity with flattery helps you to guard against it.*

After flattering his way through Nero's bloody reign, Otho took Nero's place as a promiscuously flattered emperor. He "fully understood flattery" because he "had so recently been a subject and had used the same terms." Though Kissinger "excelled at flattery and sycophancy when it came to his patrons, he found it tiresome when it was directed at him."[17]

↪ RULE 43: *Familiarity with flattery does not guarantee you can guard against it.*

Wealthy, avaricious Crassus "was most expert in winning over all men by his flatteries; on the other hand, he himself was an easy prey to flattery from anybody." Robert Dudley, Earl of Leicester, was a skillful flatterer, but his flatteries did not shield him from the flatteries of others. Rather, he was himself "gluttonous for flattery." Leicester had "the fatal defect of enjoying the flattery of his inferiors in station. Adroit intriguers burned incense to him as a god, and employed him as their tool."[18] With less vanity and more labor he could have been king of Holland; instead he died dour, disappointed, and suspected of murdering his wife.

La Rochefoucauld supposed, "If we did not flatter ourselves, the flattery of others could do us no harm."[19] Perhaps, but the situation cannot occur: we *do* flatter ourselves, badly or well, and so are vulnerable, more or less. It is vanity to suppose an attentive and inquiring soul can somehow train itself to repel flattery. No one is safe from it. "Men never shut altogether the Door against Flatterers; at most, they push it gently upon them; but they always leave it a little open."[20] The Earl of Chesterfield assured his son that "every woman is infallibly to be gained by every sort of flattery, and every man by one sort or other."[21]

⊹ RULE 44: *Warnings against flatterers flatter.*

Flattery is so flexible it takes the shape of anti-flattery (flatterers make the most of Rule 7). Colton saw it: "Some indeed there are, who profess to despise all flattery, but even these are, nevertheless, to be flattered, by being told they despise it." In *Julius Caesar* Shakespeare staged the rule: "When I tell him he hates flatterers / He says he does, being thus most flattered." Ben Jonson flattered King James by saying he could not be flattered. Flaubert defined flatterers by their eagerness to say, "By God, I cannot flatter."[22]

As the American colonies prepared to declare their independence, Aaron Burr warned a friend, "Success, promotion, the caresses of the great, and the flatteries of the low, are sometimes fatal to the noblest minds."[23] Flattery suffuses every thread of the warning, whose recipient is accorded success and promotion, caresses, flatteries, and one of the noblest minds. Because the warning was provoked by Burr's fear that his friend would be wooed away by others, it corroborates another rule:

↜ RULE 45: *Envy flatters.*

Automatic condemnation of flattery, like any automatic rejection, is stupid and lazy. Careful flattery consoles and heals. Responsible flattery lowers tension and keeps the peace. Perfect flattery is indistinguishable from the highest compliment. It will say the best words that can be said, pushing on an ego like wind behind a sail.

4. How to Flatter

> Whoever can find the means
> either by his services, his
> beauty, or his flattery, to render
> himself useful or agreeable
> to us, is sure of our affections.

DAVID HUME

3. Aesop's "Fox and Crow," by Arthur Rackham (1912) places Fox in an apparently subordinate position, which Fox uses to advantage.

In a famous fable, Crow sat in a tree with a piece of cheese in his beak. Fox saw him and said, "Crow, I'm told you have a beautiful voice. Let me hear you sing!" Crow was surprised to hear a talking fox and tickled by the compliment. He opened his mouth and cawed. The cheese fell; Fox caught it and ran away.

The fable has had a long life and many versions.[1] It is a flattery contest: like Fox [αλώπηξ], Crow (or Raven) was an emblem of flattery; in Greek, κόρακας [Raven] is only a croak removed from κόλακας [flatterer].[2] In La Fontaine's version, Fox consoles Crow that he got something in exchange for the cheese.

> You see? Be edified:
> Flatterers thrive on fool's credulity.
> The lesson's worth a cheese, don't you agree?[3]

In *Emile* (1762) Jean-Jacques Rousseau praised La Fontaine's version as "a masterpiece," then complained about it because he thought it taught a lesson in vice.[4]

↩ RULE 46: *Flattery can be taught.*

"Fox and Crow" is an ideal flattery fable: short, memorable, and full of lessons.[5] Identify what you want and who controls it; address that person with respect; discover that person's vanity and exploit it; risk nothing of your own; take what you can and scoot. The lesson is taught to Crow, but if Rousseau was right, you identify with Fox. Everyone does.

In seeming to teach about the dangers of flattery, the fable teaches its rewards. What else does it teach?

↦ RULE 47: *Thieving flattery cannot be repeated.*

If Crow learned his lesson, he won't trust Fox again.

↦ RULE 48: *Example is the best teacher. Rules alone are never enough.*

↦ RULE 49: *From simpletons all you get is cheese.*

↦ RULE 50: *Poor singers go hungry.*

↦ RULE 51: *A vain fool is a golden opportunity.*

Even if Crow had sung like a canary, he would have lost his cheese.
Finally,

↦ RULE 52: *Since opportunities are fleet and competitive, flattery must
be fast and ready.*

Rousseau teaches *à la Reynard*. He encourages competition, prizes,
and abundant praise. He examines the "dangerous but useful tool"
of selfishness. Rousseau saw that flattery comes early in education,
in and out of school. It is learned from family, folk tales, and fables.
He taught, "If you wish to teach what you have learned, geography,
mathematics, languages, music, drawing, even to find pupils, you
must have friends who will sing your praises," confirming Rules 30
and 31.[6]

↦ RULE 53: *Flattery is classical.*

Books that instruct the fine art of flattery are as ancient as Alexandria and as august as Athens and Rome. Plato analyzed flattery,
Cicero practiced it superbly, Tacitus made it a theme for history. By

Rousseau's time books that taught flattery were being written, translated, and published throughout Europe by authors of the highest repute.

⊸ RULE 54: *Flattery is philosophical.*

Emerson appreciated that "the philosopher has his value, who flatters the intellect."[7] We favor philosophers who flatter us.[8] Bias, one of the seven sages of ancient Greece, was asked to name the fiercest animal. He replied, "Of the wild animals the tyrant, and of the domesticated the flatterer." It is a wry answer with a noble pedigree.[9]

Serious study of flattery began with Socrates, who was always expert, and his pupils, who seldom were. Diogenes remarked that it was far better for Athens to fall to crows [κόρακας] than to flatterers [κόλακας].[10] Crates, a student of Diogenes, warned, "Those who live with flatterers are as defenseless as calves in the midst of wolves; for neither these nor those have any to protect them, but only such as plot against them."[11] Philodemus, a student of Zeno of Sidon, is thought to have written at least three books on flattery.[12]

We no longer have the dialogues of Aristippus, but his reputation survives. Aristippus "was capable of adapting himself to place, time, and person, and of playing his part appropriately under whatever circumstances. Hence he found more favour than anybody else with Dionysius because he could always turn the situation to good account. He derived pleasure from whatever was present, and did not toil to procure the enjoyment of something not present." If philosophy is worthwhile because it teaches how to live, Aristippus showed how philosophical flattery can be. To plead a favor for a friend, Aristippus fell at a tyrant's feet. When reproached for his abjection he responded, "It is not I who am to blame, but Dionysius who has his ears in his feet."[13]

Plato's *Gorgias* (circa 390 BC) identified four kinds of flattery (κολακεία): cooking, self-adornment, poetry, and rhetoric.[14] Most of what passes for flattery has been rhetorical, or only wordy; vigilant Plato saw long ago that it takes other shapes, too.

COOKING

From the importance of the first "dinner at my place" to the betrothal dinner, from friendship feasts to fund-raising banquets, choices of food and drink signal affection and respect. Fashionable restaurants compliment guests. Charles Ranhofer, author of *The Epicurean* (1894) and legendary chef at Delmonico's in Manhattan, "flattered the egos of those who ate at the restaurant by occasionally naming dishes after them."[15]

Flattery passes around a table like a dripping gravy boat. Plutarch observed that "kings are supposed to listen to their flatterers after dinner has begun."[16] Alexander the Great

> would begin his supper reclining on a couch, and marvelous was his care and circumspection at table, in order that everything might be served impartially and without stint; but over the wine . . . , he would sit long, for conversation's sake. And although in other ways he was of all princes most agreeable in his intercourse, and endowed with every grace, at this time his boastfulness would make him unpleasant and very like a common soldier. Not only was he himself carried away into blustering, but he suffered himself to be ridden by his flatterers. There were a great annoyance to the finer spirits in the company, who desired neither to vie with the flatterers, nor yet to fall behind them in praising Alexander. The one course they thought disgraceful, the other had its perils.[17]

⌾ RULE 55: *There is a fine line between flattery and boasting.*

SELF-ADORNMENT

Adornment is flattery at its most blatant, in your face and under your skin. The tattooed names of girlfriends, boyfriends, rock bands, bikes, corps, and Jesus are honored in living ink. Certificates give commendation tangibility and a longer life span. Perfumes are inhaled, cashmere and silk are caressed, medals, badges, and jewelry are ogled. Big girls apply dye and big boys buy big cars. Some people are downright selfish and vain, but most go to all that trouble to impress somebody else, to please them, and get a little out of that pleasing.

POETRY

Poets flatter poets generously. They dedicate poems and books to each other. Their reviews of each other shimmer like hummingbirds in honeysuckle (poetry is the hardest kind of writing to flatter without slipping in goop). Poets flatter power and famously flatter patrons. Virgil flattered Maecenas with his *Georgics*, "the best Poem of the best Poet" according to Dryden and Montaigne.[18]

Poets have praised potentates since Egypt was a pup. A papyrus from four thousand years ago hails the magical power of Pharaoh Sesostris II:

Hail to you, Khakaure, our Horus, Divine of Form!
Land's protector who widens its borders,
Who smites foreign countries with his crown.
Who holds the Two Lands in his arm's embrace,
[Who subdues foreign] lands by a motion of his hands.
Who slays Bowmen without a blow of the club,
Shoots the arrow without drawing the string.[19]

In the most ornate compliment of the English Renaissance, Edmund Spenser dedicated *The Faerie Queene* to Elizabeth I, accenting the two queens' similarities whenever he could.

In performing *Measure for Measure* on St. Stephen's Night, 1604, Shakespeare flattered King James I by alluding to the king's book of paternal advice, the *Basilikon Doron* of 1603. "In an age when flattery was a widespread accomplishment, Shakespeare was the adept. *Measure for Measure* shows him ranging the gamut from quiet flattery to fulsome. . . . A play intended as a flattery, and laden with flattery, becomes a major act of interpretation of life. Shakespeare transcends his flattery, transcends his purposes. So a poet often does."[20] August Schlegel saw in the horrors of *Macbeth* "the prudent dexterity of Shakespeare," who "could still contrive to flatter a king. . . . James the First drew his lineage from Banquo; he was the first who united the threefold sceptre of England, Scotland, and Ireland: this is foreshown in the magical vision, when a long series of glorious successors is promised to Banquo."[21]

Napoleon rewarded poets who flattered him well. "To a fellow of the name of Dagee, who sang the coronation of Napoleon the First in two hundred of the most disgusting and ill-digested lines that ever were written, containing neither metre nor sense, was assigned a place in the administration of the forest department, worth twelve thousand livres in the year—besides a present, in ready money, of one hundred napoleons d'or." Another poetaster, Brouet, presented "a long, dull, disgusting poem" which, "after comparing Bonaparte with all great men of antiquity, and *proving* that he surpasses them all, tells his countrymen that their emperor is the deputy Divinity upon earth—the mirror of wisdom, a demi-god to whom future ages will erect statues, build temples, burn incense, fall down and adore. . . . For this *delicate* compliment Brouet was made deputy postmaster-general in Italy, and a Knight of the Legion of Honor. It must be granted that, if Bonaparte is fond of flattery, he does not receive it gratis, but pays for it like a real Emperor."[22]

✦ RULE 56: *Poets are the aristocracy of flattery.*

"Ne'er / Was flattery lost on poet's ear," wrote Sir Walter Scott. With ardent flattery Clement Marot courted Marguerite de Navarre, author of the *Heptameron* and sister of King Francis I. "Marot was the king of poesy and set the fashion of wit in his time; Marguerite had a generous and a lively sympathy with wit, talent, success, renown;

the princess and the poet were mutually pleased with and flattered one another; and the liberties allowed to sympathy and flattery were great at that time."[23]

Poet to poet, Samuel Johnson held out John Dryden as the model of the "meanness and servility of hyperbolic adulation. . . . When once he has undertaken the task of praise, he no longer retains shame in himself, nor supposes it in his patron. As many odoriferous bodies are observed to diffuse perfumes from year to year, without sensible diminution of bulk or weight, he appears never to have impoverished his mint of flattery by his expenses, however lavish."[24]

Johnson complained that Dryden "made flattery too cheap. That praise is worth nothing of which the price is known."[25]

RHETORIC

Plato's *Gorgias* takes its name from Gorgias, a rhetorician whose fame endures because Plato opposed him (see Rule 6). Despite Socrates' skillful flattery, flattery and philosophy officially parted company. On occasion they reconcile.

We've come a long way since Plato; in listing only four kinds, he made a start. Flattery takes many other forms, famous ones: for instance, hope.

↬ RULE 57: *Flattery optimizes.*

A person is most susceptible to flattery when afraid, frustrated, or otherwise in need of hope. "Flattered hopes" are dashed throughout the world. Sir Philip Sidney was disappointed by "false flattering Hope." Shakespeare's Richard II growled that "cozening hope . . . is a *flatterer* / A parasite." Karl Simrock's poem "An den Mond" [To the Moon] concludes, "Only a flattering hope / keeps me together."[26] At minimum there is the hope of the flatterer, who hopes to fasten to the hopes of the flatteree. In love flattery holds hopes tenderly;

in strife it exploits them. Hope underlies all education, not least its lessons on flattery.

As Europe's capitals dickered about rules of trade, their magnates, shippers, and venders aspired to be gentlemen. Guides and manuals appeared to teach them manners. Whole chapters discussed flattery. Laurent Bordelon's *The Management of the Tongue* (1706) advised four maxims, here gratefully adopted with his commentary:

⊷ RULE 58: *"We are our first Flatterers."*

(Yes, it is a paraphrase of Rule 25, but it bears emphasis and is often repeated.) "We do certainly flatter our selves, before any Body else thinks of flattering us. . . . Are we not willing to be accounted Wise in our Actions, Exact in our Opinions, and Penetrating in our Thoughts? These are the Doors which we always keep open to Flattery."[27]

⊷ RULE 59: *"Flatterers who Praise Great Men for an imaginary merit, lull them asleep in real Miseries."*

"Great men do extremely love to flatter themselves, and consequently desire to be flattered. . . . Flatterers make themselves more odious still, by applauding the faults of those whom they flatter; by suggesting some reasons to them to justify their Injustices; by affording them some pretenses to indulge in themselves in their ill practices; and by shewing them the way of satisfying their Passions" (see Rule 106).[28]

Bordelon's mention of "great men" speaks directly to his readers, not that they need be Great Men, but that they should think they are. In a feint worthy of a grand master, he then flatters with forgiveness: "Flatterers are worse than those whom they flatter, and their Baseness is the cause of Pride and Insolence of other Men."[29] If a Great Man succumbs to flattery it is not his fault. He is excused. Furthermore:

⊷ RULE 60: *People "will often cover and flatter the defects of others, to hide their own."*

"It is true, that very often the Reason why Men flatter others, is because they desire to be flattered. By excusing the faults of others, they hope that their own will be excused."[30] Bordelon excuses himself, excuses everybody. After all,

⊷ RULE 61: *No one "ought to avoid the Character of a Flatterer so as to become brutish."*

"All those, who out of an affected niceness of Conscience, will never praise any Body, are commonly insupportable in the commerce of the World."[31] People who do not praise are not popular. People who do not flatter do not praise enough.

A popular eighteenth-century anthology, *Instructions for Youth, Gentlemen and Noblemen*, gathered four texts by Sir Walter Raleigh, Lord Treasurer Burleigh, Cardinal Sermonetta, and Edward Walsingham. The anthology's editor told readers that Walsingham's *Manual of Prudential Maxims for Statesmen and Courtiers* "crowns all, and is thought to be the Performance of some unfortunate Spanish Minister in his Retirement, and we are indebted to Mr. Walsingham (whose name it bears) for the Excellent and Masterly Translation." To sell books the publisher flattered Walsingham's translation blindly, since without an original text he could not know how masterly the translation was.[32]

The *Manual* disdained abuse of flattery, to do it justice. Its chapter 7 explains why "if you live in Court, you must sometimes so flatter the Prince, as may gain him unto you." The *Manual* counsels against overdoing praise: "he whom we flatter too grossly, suspects Deceit" (see Rule 12). It recommends a blending of truth and creativity: "It is requisite still that Flattery have something of Truth, and some Show of Liberty mixed with it, (it is the Opinion of *Aeschines* and *Plutarch*) whereby we may persuade not only the Prince that we speak heartily, and as we think, but others also, and so preserve our Credit"[33] (Rule 9). To gain anything else, flattery must first gain access. Means are always available — namely truths, selected and brought to a shine.

↜ RULE 62: *Flattery gains an audience in which other things can be said.*

Dupont de Nemours wrote to Thomas Jefferson that Napoleon's ministers kept their places "only by flattering his military pride," a precondition for offering advice.[34] "First placate, then lead," advises the *Shih chi* (Rule 91).[35] Refined flattery is as discreet as an envelope. Flatfooted flattery crashes like a waiter's tray.

If you don't want much, you don't need to flatter much to see what good it will do you. If you want a great deal and expect flattery to help you, don't expect flattery to be some kind of magic: a few well-chosen words and poof! You're promoted! It's not that easy. To flatter a person's wardrobe, car, home, furniture, and the like places the flatteree at a respectful distance. To get close to a flatteree, close enough to touch, a flatterer practices six essential exercises:

1. HYGIENE. The most potent compliment will fizzle if uttered with stench or visible spittle.

2. TASTE. A flatterer should notice if a flatteree prefers gray or blue, salt or sweet, Fox News or Sheryl Crow. Snooping sets off alarms; study flatters.

3. CONVIVIALITY. A foxy flatterer will need to slip between other flatterers and apply preliminary flattery to each. Watch how others flatter and how the potentate reacts.

4. CIRCUMSPECTION. In many cases a presumed potentate may be a mere figurehead, with real power emanating from a subordinate, or from several. Stifle advice about choosing your enemies; they'll choose you soon enough.

5. SURVEY. A flatterer should measure perimeters. At what distance does the flatteree cease to hear well? At what point does the flatteree pay no attention? If you want your flattery to take you far, remember Machiavelli and his Prince, going high up a hill to get the broad view.

6. TIMING. The best compliments linger. A flatterer will briefly prolong a farewell, express the honeyed phrase, and leave it as a last impression, more likely to last, more likely to be savored. Be quick, but don't hurry. Take your time: if you can't take strides, take steps.

↤ RULE 63: *To reach high or deep a flatterer needs time, or many times.*

Timing is everything. Constraint is as vital as expression: not too soon, not too fast, not too much. Patience is foxy.

↤ RULE 64: *Flattery does not always seek immediate reward.*

Potentates are besieged by clumsy flatterers who flatter, then ask for something. This can spoil the pleasure of the flattery and doom the flatterer. When possible, flatter the potentate without asking for anything at all. Then, when the time comes to ask for a favor, accompanying flattery will be more credible.

Put aside the fable that a flatterer leads the languid life of a parasite, solely devoted to sucking its host. Such a flatterer is a bottom feeder, no more worthy of attention than a carp. The parasitical flatterer dies miserably, rightfully despised by all, most of all by successful flatterers. Successful flatterers, the ones most worth study, are careful, loyal, honest, and ever vigilant for the safety and strength of their flatterees.

↝ RULE 65: *Flatterers identify with their flatterees.*

In the flames of Russia's 1905 revolution, Leo Shestov saw one of vanity's favorite feints: "To praise oneself is considered improper, immodest; to praise one's own sect, one's own philosophy, is considered the highest duty."[36]

Louis Antoine Fauvelet de Bourrienne had been Napoleon's classmate at military school, remained his friend through his climb to power, and in 1797 became his private secretary. In his *Memoirs* he describes Napoleon in 1801 beset by flatterers. "Truth now reached him with difficulty, and when it was not agreeable he had no disposition to hear it. He was surrounded by flatterers; and, the greater number of those who approached him, far from telling him what they really thought, only repeated what he had himself been thinking."[37] From Bourrienne's point of view Napoleon succumbed to his flatterers, and it is they who must take the blame. For what? For agreeing.

↝ RULE 66: *Silence flatters.*

"Even a fool, when he holdeth his peace, is counted wise," says the Proverb (17:28). Agreement is flattery's favorite environment. Well-timed nods flatter. In a pinch,

↝ RULE 67: *Flatterers take blame.*

Samuel Adams remarked of King George III, "Why should we cast the odium of distressing Mankind upon his Minions & Flatterers only. Guilt must lie at his Door."[38] But this was exceptional. Cunning potentates gather flatterers purposely in order to blame them when policies fail.[39] A standard opinion about Napoleon held that "but for the base servility of his flatterers, and the approbation of a whole people deceived by the eulogiums of a perfidious and venal court, he would have been a good prince."[40]

Bourrienne's account of an autocrat surrounded by chiefs is an inevitability. In a cabinet where the potentate's opinions are unanimously approved, wise flatterers will supply them ready-made. It is easy and honest to assent to opinions you have already crafted. Bourrienne portrays an insecure Napoleon whose every whim is endorsed. Why?

In 1802 Bourrienne was disgraced by a procurement scandal and sharply dismissed. Because he had a score to settle and because Napoleon was safely dead, his *Memoirs* (published in ten volumes between 1829 and 1831) are suspect. According to Baron de Méneval, Bourrienne's *Memoirs* were put together by his publisher and ghostwriters hired to ruin Napoleon's reputation.[41]

Méneval, Napoleon's secretary after Bourrienne, wrote his own *Memoirs* in the mid-1840s, describing a very different administration: Napoleon surrounded himself most deliberately with "a rare composition of eminent and varied talents," some of whom he trusted less than others. According to Méneval, at meetings of the Council of State "discussion was perfectly free; each Councillor of State had the right to express his opinion, whatever it might be." Napoleon "even provoked contradiction, protesting that all he desired was to be enlightened. It sometimes occurred that he yielded to the opinion of the majority, whilst declaring himself, however, unconvinced."[42]

Both could be right. It is perfectly possible that Napoleon's cabinet was led by highly competent men who were flatterers, and who sometimes got their way despite Napoleon's better judgment. All that is needed to reconcile the two accounts is recognition of a plain fact: powerful people accustomed to flattery are sometimes able to deal with it. They can feel so much at ease with it that they can enjoy it for its own sake.

❧ RULE 68: *Flattery does not need to fool to be effective.*

In September 1808 Napoleon was at the height of his imperial career. He entered Erfurt, Germany, as a conqueror come to decide the fate of nations. He was immediately surrounded by flatterers. Talleyrand reported, "My duties as grand chamberlain enabled me to see the forced, simulated, or even sincere homage which was rendered to Napoleon, more than I could have done otherwise, and gave it proportions which appeared to me monstrous. Never did baseness display so much genius."[43] Yet Napoleon took it in stride and went about his business.

At Erfurt Napoleon greeted the rulers of Europe to set his conditions for peace. An honored guest was Czar Alexander I, a man whose company he enjoyed, and whose nation he had not yet invaded. On the eve of negotiations about the end of war in Europe, they talked about their wives, but even family talk reverted to empire. Attuned to Napoleon's hints and aspirations, Czar Alexander flattered him to the heart, suggesting that he divorce Josephine and marry into a legitimate royal family, his own. He offered him the Grand-Duchess Anna, then in her teens.[44] It was an idea Napoleon embraced — for the sake of Europe, of course.

As a witness to this dinner, Talleyrand praised the quality of the conversation of the two emperors, in sharp contrast to the crudeness of Germany's little kings. "If victory brings into his dominions, into his very palace, a man before whom he can himself be but a courtier, he will stoop, in the presence of his victor, as low as he wished his own subjects to do before himself. He cannot conceive any other form of flattery. At powerful courts, they know another means of raising themselves: it is to bow; petty princes only know how to crawl."[45]

❧ RULE 69: *Flatterers shift positions.*

"It is possible to be below flattery as well as above it," said Baron Macaulay.[46] The worst of it cannot rise and the best of it can be squandered.

A sensible flatterer considers whether it is better to speak first or last, up or down, and how long to hold forth. When King Arthur proposed war with Rome, Hoel the Great, king of Armorica, quickly subordinated: "Even if every one of us were to take the trouble to turn all these things over in his mind and to reconsider each point deep within himself, it is my opinion that no one could find better advice to give than what has just emerged from your own experienced and highly-skilled wisdom. Your speech, adorned as it was with Ciceronian eloquence, has anticipated exactly what we all think. We should have nothing but unstinting praise for the opinion expressed by so steadfast a man as you."[47]

As reported by Geoffrey of Monmouth, Hoel's speech is flattery warm and thick. It assents to King Arthur's decision, praises how he reached it, praises his experience, wisdom, and eloquence, claims to praise him in the name of all, and thereby makes it exceedingly difficult for anyone else to exceed or contradict him. No one did.

Hoel's example illustrates the pride of place. He dares to speak first and to flatter because he is Hoel, a king himself, and a renowned warrior. Crude flattery from him would mean more to King Arthur than polished compliments from a lesser man.

❧ RULE 70: *Flattery is status conscious.*

Hoel's flattery is of a very high order, since he had earned command in battle and maneuver. Arthur would hear a firm pledge of loyalty within the flattery, an example of the kind that parasites parrot in the hope of being taken as seriously as Hoel.

A serious flatterer soon learns not to waste good flattery on dull ears. A good flatterer, if merely good, ought to be able to get the flatteree to acknowledge good flattery, by thanks, reward, or by asking for more. A smile, a laugh, or reciprocal flattery signals a happy competence. A superior flatterer, well rounded, sensitive, and tasteful, as few other than you can be, will express flattery so pure and rich as to please the flatteree unto ecstasy, stimulating an eagerness to hear again, even say aloud, that excellent flattery. An excellent flatterer will not rely on words alone.

↤ RULE 71: *Gifts flatter.*

In *Leviathan* (1651), the hardheaded realist Thomas Hobbes counseled, "To give great gifts to a man, is to honour him; because it is buying of protection, and acknowledging of power. To give little gifts, is to dishonour; because it is but alms, and signifies an opinion of the need of small helps. To be sedulous in promoting another's good; also to flatter, is to honour; as a sign we seek his protection or aid."[48]

"Just praise is only a debt," Samuel Johnson decided, "but flattery is a present." Beethoven wrote: "The world is a king, and, like a king, desires flattery in return for favor; but true art is stubborn — it will not submit to the mold of flattery."[49] Rather than compose flattering art, he composed as best he could, then flattered friends and potentates by dedicating works to them. He improvised the art of giving art.

In his 1844 essay "Gifts" Emerson recommended fruit and flowers. "Men use to tell us that we love flattery, even though we are not deceived by it, because it shows that we are of importance enough to be courted. Something like that pleasure, the flowers give us."[50]

↤ RULE 72: *Really big flattery gives really big gifts.*

Lovers give themselves, flattering themselves that they give more than they get. Daughters and daughters with dowries are ritually given in marriage. Any parent who would surrender a daughter for the sake of flattering a prince, and any prince who would consent to such flattery, should recall the examples of Mademoiselle d'Aumale and Catherine the Great. One became queen of Portugal and the other empress of Russia, both by marrying vain men and outmaneuvering them. Girl-giving parents can flatter themselves that they have given a priceless gift to the potentate, but what about the girl? Mademoiselle Fontanges was given to King Louis XIV "by her shameless family" and endured the king's ardor for months till she died in childbirth.[51]

-ᘐ RULE 73: *Money flatters.*

Money is versatile, able at once to be the goal of flattery and a means for flattering further. A patron flatters an artist by paying more than the asking price. In politics the power of money to turn heads and win friends is so great it trips alarms. A campaign donation is flattery with a precise value.

-ᘐ RULE 74: *Fortune flatters.*

Potentates flatter themselves that good luck is proof of God's favor, bad luck is just bad luck. Skeptical self-regarding Nietzsche spoke from experience: "We do not dispute what is magical or irrational when it flatters our self-esteem."[52] His autobiography, *Ecce Homo* (1888), has chapters titled "Why I Am So Wise" and "Why I Am So Clever." Why was Nietzsche so favored? Genetics and geography. Which reminds me: How unique you are! How fortunate that you were born in your native land instead of some foreign place! How fortunate I am to find you!

Benjamin Disraeli became prime minister of England in 1868. He lavished flattery. Lord Russell recalled that Disraeli "succeeded in converting the dislike with which he had once been regarded in the highest quarters with admiration and even affection, by his elaborate and studied acquiescence in every claim, social or political, of Royalty, and by his unflagging perseverance in the art of flattery." Disraeli advised Matthew Arnold, "Everyone likes flattery; and when you come to Royalty you should lay it on with a trowel."[53]

Flattery is literally laid on with a trowel. It builds monuments and mansions, stone by stone. In Italy Nietzsche learned that "architecture is a kind of eloquence of power in forms—now persuading, even flattering, now only commanding."[54] A palace loses much of its pleasure if no one envies it. An invitation to visit is a form of praise perfectly imitated by flattery. In every generation there are rulers of real estate, able to give away tracts and houses. Their capacity for generosity is so extensive they can flatter with the landscape. Napoleon gave one of his brothers Holland, and another Spain.

Cities and towns are named after Caesars and presidents, roads and boulevards are named after bankers and businessmen, buildings are named after martyrs, tycoons, and coaches.

❖ RULE 75: *Architecture flatters.*

Madame de Montespan, always good for a story, tells in her *Secret Memoirs* how Nicolas Fouquet, superintendent of finances, invited King Louis XIV to his home at Vaux-le-Vicomte. "It was a veritable fairy palace. All in this brilliant dwelling was stamped with the mark of opulence and of exquisite taste in art." King Louis there discovered the paintings of Charles Le Brun, whom he would bring to Versailles to commemorate his glory. Louis admired the estate from his balcony, approved its perspective and its placement of pavilions and side buildings, but pointed out a vista spoiled by white clearings. Voilà! Overnight Fouquet employed gardeners and diggers so that, when the king stepped out to his balcony the next morning, "he saw a beautiful green wood in place of the clearings." Fouquet expected the king to be impressed; instead he was outraged and shouted, "I am shocked at such expense!" Fouquet was fired, arrested, and imprisoned.[55] Fouquet crossed a line that's hard to see, where flattery turns into bragging (Rule 55). He needed to study flattery, specifically Plutarch:

> Valerius [later known as Publicola] was living in a very splendid house on the so-called Velia. It hung down over the Forum, commanded a view of all that passed there, and was surrounded by steeps and hard to get at, so that when he came down from it the spectacle was a lofty one, and the pomp of his procession was worthy of a king. Accordingly, Valerius showed what a good thing it is for men in power and high station to have ears which are open to frankness and truth instead of flattery. For when he heard from his friends, who spared him no detail, that he was thought by the multitude to be transgressing, he was not obstinate nor exasperated, but quickly got together a large force of workmen, and while it was still night tore the house down, and razed it all to the ground. In the morning, therefore, the Romans saw what had happened, and came flocking together. They were moved to love and admiration by the man's magnanimity.[56]

⍩ RULE 76: *Names flatter.*

Children are named after relatives, patron saints, and celebrities. Time itself is not safe: perpetual memorials to Caesars were incorporated into the calendar: Quintilis became July and Sextilis became August. "The senate urged upon Tiberius the request that the month of November, on the sixteenth day of which he had been born, should be called Tiberius; but he replied: 'What will you do, then, if there are thirteen Caesars?' "[57] Subsequent Caesars were less modest. A slavish Roman senate offered to move the beginning of the New Year forward a month in order to honor Nero, who was born in December. Nero declined the honor but later renamed April as Neroneus, a novelty that died with him.[58] Antoninus Pius refused renaming months in honor of his wife and himself, but Commodus wrought havoc, consenting to the renaming the calendar in his honor, driving out July to put Commodus before August.[59]

↬ RULE 77: *The dead flatter.*

The dead have been summoned to flatter the living. Genealogies of King Numa were forged "to gratify the pride of certain persons by inserting their names among the first families and the most illustrious houses." Gibbon disputed the history of the Egyptian priest Manetho and despised the "flattering genealogists" of Elagabulus. "Flattery is the prolific parent of falsehood, and falsehood, I will now add, is not incompatible with the sacerdotal character. Manetho's history of Egypt is dedicated to Ptolemy Philadelphus, who derived a fabulous or illegitimate pedigree from the Macedonian kings of the race of Hercules."[60]

↬ RULE 78: *Intelligence flatters.*

When in doubt, flatter intelligence. All of us want to believe we show flashes of genius (see Rules 20 and 22). In college Ted Kooser liked to walk around campus with a copy of Kierkegaard's *Fear and Trembling* tucked under his arm because he thought it looked good and attracted women (see Rules 38 and 54).[61]

"The Seductress," a poem from the Dead Sea Scrolls, warns that the seductress

> is ever prompt to oil her words,
> And she flatters with irony.[62]

What an insightful little text this is! It adds important information about the seductress (described at length in chapter 7 of Proverbs): her ordnance includes irony, a weapon most effective against intellectuals.

Flattery requires a thorough study of vanity, but by no means should it stop there. Vanity is infamously prone to error. Flattery also requires a thorough study of virtue because (1) virtue is good; and (2) for every virtue there is a vanity.

❧ RULE 79: *Every good deed that can be praised can be fluttered.*

The flatterer who most readily ascertains virtues and distinguishes their degree will sooner find and please a worthy flatteree. Thus do flatterers assemble, thus do saints distrust disciples. Excepting the stingy and stupid, flatterees treasure nothing more than their virtues, and treasure most of all the virtues they believe are most securely theirs.

Like most political discourse, flattery stirs suspicion: it hides ugly truth, it mingles in gossip, it competes with outright lies, it can be terribly embarrassing, and it suffers in the hands of hacks. For grumpuses who suppose that history is just one blunder after another, the history of flattery shows progress.

❧ RULE 80: *Flattery is professionalized.*

Rome invented the profession of paid flatterer. In the reign of Tiberius a mediocre speaker, Larcius Licinius, introduced the claque — people paid to applaud and cheer — a symptom that forecast the art of eloquence would soon be dead. When he performed in public Nero "got ready a special corps of about five thousand soldiers, called Augustans; these would lead the applause, and all the rest, however loath, were obliged to shout with them."[63]

Some flatteries are as necessary and disposable as tissue or toilet water. The flattery paid to a functionary may be token, but a flattering potentate knows tokens are cheaply paid, and pays them. Confucius said, "Tokens and titles — these alone must not be lightly handed out. It is the duty of the ruler to see to that. Titles create trust, and trust insures the proper use of tokens."[64]

↭ RULE 81: *Flattery is a means of administration.*

To explain how a well-ordered state arranges ranks and duties, Charles Loyseau's *Treatise of Orders and Plain Dignities* (1610) traced the place of "honorary" offices back to the Justinian Code. "The available offices were hardly enough to suit and accommodate all those who wanted them. So the emperors invented plain dignities," honor adorned with insignia, pomp cloaking impotence.[65] Wherever rank is emphasized, the potentate has greater power to use flattery.

To assess taxes and grant exemptions, Louis XIV imposed 568 degrees of social distinction, a system that created great rivalries over small differences, and in which a modest promotion could divert a whole court in a frenzy of jealousy.[66] In 1689, again at war, Louis decided it was time to award a large number of Blue Ribbons, the *Cordons bleus* of the Order of the Holy Ghost. "There was a large number of promotions: seventy-three, in fact. Those who had taken part in the war had a considerable share in them, for it was seen that their services would be required again, and that other rewards would be more expensive."[67]

Napoleon created the Legion of Honor in order to create his own bureau of prestige. As with the Cordons bleus, the legion proved to be a useful dispensary for flattery in lieu of more substantial compensation. At Mentz "no Prince or Minister fawned more assiduously upon Bonaparte" than the Baron Edelsheim, "the most inoffensive and least dangerous of all imbecile creatures that ever entered the Cabinet of a Prince." Bonaparate asked Talleyrand, "What can Edelsheim mean by his troublesome assiduities? Does he want any indemnities, or does he wish me to make him a German Prince?" Talleyrand replied that the baron coveted admission to the Legion of Honor. "Nothing else?" said Napoleon and, as if relieved of an oppressive burden, bought the baron's adoration with a ribbon.[68]

Against power and diffidence, demands and presumption, a flatterer seeks out the flatteree's cherished pride. Rev. Croxall commented, "Let the ambuscade be disposed with due judgment, and it will scarce fail of seizing the most guarded heart. How many are tickled to the last degree with the pleasure of flattery, even while they are applauded for their honest detestation of it!"[69]

Fox likes a Crow with a fine opinion of itself.

Anethum Fœniculum

Published by W. Woodville, August 1. 1792.

EMBLEMS OF FLATTERY

4. In Elizabethan England fennel was an emblem
of flattery. Tudor herbals recommended it as a
remedy for scorpion stings, dog bites, constipation,
and gas. Ophelia gives fennel to Laertes: "There's
fennel for you, and columbines" (*Hamlet*, 4.5.181).

Scire cupis dominos toties cur Thessalis ora
Mutet, et ut varios quaerat habere duces?
Nescit adulari, cuiquamve obtrudere palpum,
Regia quem morem Principis omnis habet.
Sed veluti ingenuus sonipes, dorso excutit omnem,
Qui moderari ipsum nesciat Hippocomon.
Nec saevire tamen domino fas: ultio sola est,
Dura ferum ut iubeat ferre lupata magis.

5. "In Adulari Nescientem" [On One Who Knows Not to Flatter], 1600. Andrea Alciati's *Emblemata* included two emblems of flattery: type and antitype. He gives the antitype first: the beast that does not know how to flatter, shown here. His poem asks and answers: "Do you want to know why Thessaly changes masters so often and why it seeks to have different leaders? Because it does not know how to flatter, how to coax, in the fashion of the court of every prince. Instead, like a wild steed, it bucks off every rider unable to control it. Yet the master should not be angry: the only recourse is to command the beast to endure a harder bit." *Emblemata* was exceedingly popular: more than 175 editions appeared in the sixteenth and seventeenth century. The emblem is aristocratic: anyone who cannot or will not flatter is a beast.

Semper hiat, semper tenuem, qua vescitur, auram
Reciprocat Chamaeleon:
Et mutat faciem, varios sumitque colores,
Praeter rubrum vel candidum.
Sic et adulator populari vescitur aura,
Hiansque cuncta devorat:
Et solum mores imitatur Principis atros
Albi et pudici nescius.

6. "*In Adulatores*" [On Flatterers], an emblem from Alciati's *Emblemata* (1542) depicts the stereotype: a chameleon. The poem explains:

"Always gaping, it is forever breathing in and out the thin air on which it feeds; it changes its appearance, assumes different colors, except for red or white. So does the flatterer feed on the air of popularity, and, gaping, devours all; he imitates only the vicious habits of the prince, incapable of the pure and the chaste." Plutarch established the chameleon as a flattery emblem ("How to Tell a Flatterer from a Friend," 287). The chameleon lore comes from Pliny's *Natural History,* 8.120–21.

Illustrations of "In Adulatores" for three different editions of Alciati's *Emblemata* depict an evolving imaginary chameleon. Like flattery, it changes with the scene.

7. 1548

8. 1608

9. 1639

✧ Peacock:

"I may truly say of the flatterer, *Pavo est*; hee is a Peacock; for *hee hath the colour of an Angell, the *pace of a thiefe, and voice of a devill*" (14).

✧ Dog:

"It is a *fawning* vice, too; *dog-like*, who *fawnes* upon his *Master* for crusts and bones. . . . Hee uses his *mouth* as the dogge waggs his *tayle*, the one to *obtaine* a *boone* from his *friend*, the other to *gaine* a *bone* from his *Master*" (16).

Henry Harflete's *The Hunting of the Fox; or, Flattery Displayed* (1632) proposes several emblems for a flatterer, most often the fox. At the start of the book he forecasts that he'll "rip open the belly of the fox-flatterer." He then offers one emblem after another.

⪔ VV:

"Of all letters in the *Crosse-row* a VV is the worst, for
it is a dissembling and flattering knaves *Epitheton*. . . .
Flattery and hypocrisie keepe their *revells* in that
heart, where the figure of a *double tongue* hangs at the
doore of the mouth: The embleme of deceit" (43–44).

⪔ Rat:

"Would you have the *Embleme* of a *flatterer*? I have
read of *Trochylus* the little Wren of *Egypt*, who doth
picke the Crocodiles teeth, whereby he doth feed
himselfe, this tickling and pleasing of the bird doth
cause him to gape wide, which *Ichneumon* the *Rat* of
Pharaoh perceiving, and taking her advantage by
this meanes, shooteth suddainly into the bowells of
the Crocodile, and eateth out his belly" (53).

⪔ Monster:

· "Beware of this *flatterer*, for hee is a monster. . . .
a head like an Oxe, a backe like an Asse, to bear
all taunts, *a belly like a Hogge* to drink with all
companies, and a *tayle* like a *dogge* to fawne upon
every comer" (72).

10. Reynard the courtier, by
Wilhelm von Kaulbach
(1846).

11. Pious Reynard, by Gustav
Jacob Canton (1852).

12. Lord High Chancellor Reynard, by A. T. Elwes (1873).

5. The Flatteree

Flattery is a fine pick-lock
of tender ears; especially of
those whom fortune hath
borne high upon their wings.

BEN JONSON

Like other precious skills — music, languages, friendship — flattery is best perfected if practiced from childhood. A child's compliment is pure delight. If flattery were the worst vice tried by teens, parents would age slower.

Youth has two grand advantages: plenty of opportunity and more likelihood that goofs will be forgiven and forgotten. Learning the types, styles, and tricks of flattery helps achieve proficiency, but practice, and much of it, separates the fox from the badgers. Through practice an aspiring flatterer finds the pitch that cuts through static. With practice flatterers build repertoire.

↦ RULE 82: *Practice perfects a flatterer.*

Practice enables a flatterer to interpret and react instantly. Flatterers adjust for the flatteree and the occasion: purpose, place, lighting, acoustics, weather, time and time limit, number and nature of witnesses. When flattery is well practiced and closely watched it can be played as formally as a game, in singles, doubles, and teams. Speed and stamina succeed. Amateurs imitate champions.

↦ RULE 83: *Flatterees are easy to find.*

"There are few so low but find some body to cajole and flatter them."[1] A little puff inflates a pupa into a potentate. Aristotle explained that "most men, because they love honour, seem to be more desirous of receiving than of bestowing affection. Hence most men like flattery."[2] And women? They treat flattery as a token of taste, intellect, motive, and charm. In 1938 Marjorie Bowen supposed that "the praise of ladies is hardly flattery."[3] (In 1938 it hardly mattered.) If a potentate presumes praise is due, a flatterer supplies it, due or not.

In the ceaseless struggle for the top of the heap, signs of superiority, no matter how slight, flimsy, or counterfeit, are facts of life. They spur ambition and fantasies. They itch, nag, wheedle, and provoke. You know better, you deserve more, you should be famous, you should be in charge.

At home or on the job most people don't get to choose their flatterees. The world provides them: relatives, teachers, preachers, a big boss, a bigger boss, bankers, judges, uptight clerks, and uniformed officers. Thus, a hard rule:

⤙ RULE 84: *A skillful flatterer can flatter anybody.*

A foxy flatterer quickly gets a fix on the work required. Sad to say, not every potentate can be flattered, and many can be flattered only by a chosen few who, by breeding, manner, and status, are allowed to approach. Easy pickings is a person like Nixon who needs flattery frequently; a person who needs none will be brutish and not worth the trouble. A person who needs just a little flattery is the best test for a flatterer, but it is no more than a test. The proof of attainment lies in the reward (Rule 10), and the reward depends on the flatteree. The more the flatteree can give, the more the flatterer will try to get it. What did Rome teach Gibbon?

⤙ RULE 85: *"Flattery adheres to power."*[4]

Tolstoy presumed that intrigue, deceit, flattery, and self-deception are "inseparable from power," so much so that some rulers come to crave flattery, some to despise it. Tiberius hated flattery, Galba scorned it, Marcus Aurelius praised his father because he was "deaf to flattery." Severus Alexander ejected flatterers from his presence and submitted them to ridicule.[5] Bismarck admired Kaiser Wilhelm I for repelling flatterers. "No one would have dared to flatter him openly to his face. In his feeling of royal dignity he would have thought, 'if any one had the right of praising me to my face, he would also have the right of blaming me to my face.'"[6] But one potentate's poison is another's apéritif: Julius Caesar, Napoleon, and Catherine the Great lapped up flattery like honey without diminishing their judgment or authority.

Flattery circulates in the commerce of empires. It divides, rules, and ranks. It is downright righteous.

↬ RULE 86: *Flattery is a duty.*

It is enforced by law. Official signs of respect due to an official (whether respected or not) are functional flattery, exceedingly useful for setting tone, avoiding contempt, and suppressing spite. When a potentate wants flattery, those who want the potentate's regard will provide plenty of it. The sooner citizens learn flattery's formalities the more they can play.

The highest of the high are often out of sight and out of reach. They may live far away and speak a different language. They keep to their class and flatter each other with hospitality and intermarriage. The most fortunate flatterers orbit extraordinary people whose accomplishments deserve recognition.

↬ RULE 87: *Contempt flatters.*

In *Gil Blas* Le Sage proposed that "a sycophant may run any risk with the great, who swallow all kinds of flattery, let it be ever so absurd."[7] The proposal is itself absurd, but it suits his purpose perfectly: it flatters his readers, for whom a book is as close to the great as they're likely to get, and for whom the distance is a blessing, thank you very much (Rule 45). Next in line, battening fat, are the flatterers of the would-be great.

⟜ RULE 88: *"None are more taken in by flattery than the proud, who wish to be the first and are not."*

So wrote Spinoza.[8] The bigger the ego, the bigger the appetite for flattery, but prudent potentates seek to conceal the craving and indulge it privately (Rule 22). To enhance its value, a flatterer needs to dole out flattery selectively, as if it matters, in intimate occasions when a flatteree is free to enjoy the best of the best.

Some compliments shine in privacy, some need crowds and amplifiers. It is not necessary to speak directly to a potentate to flatter. An adept flatterer can flatter an absent potentate through gossip, print, radio, and TV (Rule 19).

⟜ RULE 89: *Flatteries are building blocks of fame.*

Most people have bosses. When we talk with them we watch our tongues; when we talk about them anything is possible, including sheer fiction. We polish or scratch their reputations. We give them glory, mediocrity, or grief. They stand aloof but cannot stand apart: their lives, like ours, are full of uncertainty. Their confidence and performance are bound up to some degree with ours. How should we address them? What should we embellish and what should we suppress?

Our bosses are sober, sensitive, and wise, and the more powerful they are the more accustomed they are to flattery (Rule 17). They crush poor flatterers like bugs. They respect responsibility, support science and art, and uphold standards. The best potentate is an alert potentate, who appraises and appreciates our actions and reactions, our salvaging, our insights, our loyalty, our strength. A flatterer may have the good luck to serve a potentate who cares about the flatterer's welfare, but if not, if the potentate is tuned to a different frequency and steering away, then what can a flatterer do to attract the potentate's attention?

There are a thousand things a flatterer can do to win a potentate's regard, but a thousand are too many to list or remember. Here are the top ten.

1. Emulate the potentate.[9]
2. Be visibly diligent in your labor.
3. Cheer up the potentate. "A good report maketh the bones fat," says Proverbs (15:30).[10]
4. Protect the potentate's posterior.
5. Remember that your potentate answers to a higher potentate. Your good flattery could elevate your potentate; it could work its way up.
6. Do not pester the potentate.
7. Do not try to fool the potentate.
8. Do not consort with bad flatterers.
9. Face high water, endure hard times, take heat.
10. When all goes well, celebrate the potentate's genius. When times are tough, assure the potentate that come what may, your devoted counsel is there for the asking.

A flatterer can get to know the potentate by trial and error as time goes by, but the fastest and safest means is flattery. Except for codgers like Tiberius and Galba, potentates do not despise flattery. Some are shameless gluttons and some are connoisseurs. Higher potentates know flattery of every quality and application, accepting it as a privilege of rank. They measure their status by the quality of their flatterers. "He that loves to be flattered is worthy o' the flatterer," quoth Shakespeare.[11]

Away from potentates and in pursuit of happiness, a flatterer will seek and treasure tender opportunities. Flattery flutters about courtship and soars in true romance. Courtship gives a flatterer a chance to choose a flatteree, or several chances. Lovesick men are such suckers for flattery that a few vague hints about a special something can seduce them. Philaenis of Samos's handbook on love instructed its readers how to flatter a woman: tell her she is sexy, say she is fascinating, call her a "wild pigeon."[12]

↬ RULE 90: *"I love you" is without rival the most beloved and abused of flatteries.*

"You flatter yourself" is a ready reply.

Cleopatra was reputed to have a thousand forms of flattery, none too few for the most famous seductress in history.[13] When she and Caesar flirted they had a flattery jamboree.

If the flatteree is a lover — or a possible lover — the flatterer will want to devote breath and lips to better use than talking, but the importance of fine phrases for sparking, sustaining, and enhancing romance cannot be taken lightly. Elegance is charming, compliments establish goodwill, and original flattery, precisely fit and custom tinted for the flatteree, has the advantage of surprise in overcoming defenses. Praise lingers longer than perfume.

Choice quotations from famous films and poems show playfulness and sophistication (Rule 78). Chinese literature abounds in dialogues that hang on a person's ability to quote spontaneously and to the point. But quotations run the risk of appearing pompous or derivative. Old ways are often the best ways. Flatterers advance, murmuring, "I need you," "I miss you," "I want you."

And enemies?

↬ RULE 91: *Flattery placates.*

Tocqueville asks, "After the fact of hating their enemies, what is more natural to men than flattering them?"[14]

A flatterer can always hope that mollifying flattery will eventually lead to triumph and revenge. Saint-Simon licked the boots of the Abbé Dubois, but later had the pleasure of spitting on his grave.[15] Scipion Dupleix "flattered the Queen of Navarre during her lifetime and wrote a satire on her after her death."[16] Shostakovich eluded as best he could the pressure to dedicate one of his works to Stalin, till in 1949 he hastily wrote the music for *Song of the Forests*, a cantata that sang "Glory to the Party of Lenin! Glory to the People forever! Glory to the wise Stalin, Glory!" Upon Stalin's death and discrediting, he removed the lines.[17]

✧ RULE 92: *Flattery is political.*

It goes up or down. When flattery falls flat the flatterer falls, too. When it reaches a higher plane and catches hold, it can pull itself up and start anew. Politicians flatter professionally (Rule 80).

Flatterers are reviled for fawning on potentates and potentates are blamed for believing them. Juvenal exclaimed, "There is nothing that divine Majesty will not believe concerning itself when lauded to the skies!"[18] In republics the roles reverse, or seem to. George Bernard Shaw observed that "the politician who once had to learn how to flatter Kings has now to learn how to fascinate, amuse, coax, humbug, frighten, or otherwise strike the fancy of the electorate."[19] Republicans and Democrats, look to your precedents! After studying democracies, tyrannies, oligarchies, and empires, Plutarch chides rulers twice: for succumbing to flattery and for flattering the crowd.[20]

✧ RULE 93: *Democracy abets flattery.*

Fear of flattery is a constant companion of fear of democracy. Aristotle warned that democracies degenerate into tyrannies when the public becomes accustomed to flattery. "The demagogue is the flatterer of the people."[21] In the run-up to the American Revolution, Samuel Adams reminded Boston patriots of a favorite example:

> Had not *Caesar* seen that Rome was *ready to stoop*, he would not have dared to make himself the master of that once brave people.

He was indeed, as a great writer observes, a *smooth* and *subtle* tyrant, who led them gently into slavery; "and on his brow, o'er daring vice deluding virtue smil'd." By pretending to be the people's greatest friend, he gain'd the ascendency over them: By beguiling arts, hypocrisy and flattery, which are even more fatal than the sword, he obtain'd that supreme power which his ambitious soul had long thirsted for: The people were finally prevail'd upon to *consent* to their own ruin: By the force of perswasion, or rather by cajoling arts and tricks always made use of by men who have ambitious views.[22]

Stengel found the fear of flattery openly discussed in debates about the making of the American Constitution.[23]

With an eye on modern states, Edmund Burke predicted: "When the leaders choose to make themselves bidders at an auction of popularity, their talents, in the construction of the state, will be of no service. They will become flatterers instead of legislators." And in another context: "As to the people at large, when once these miserable sheep have broken the fold, and have got themselves loose, not from the restraint, but from the protection, of all the principles of natural authority and legitimate subordination, they become the natural prey of impostors. When they have once tasted of the flattery of knaves, they can no longer endure reason, which appears to them only in the form of censure and reproach."[24]

Nietzsche scorned partisan elections that flatter "all those who would like to *seem* independent and individual, as if they fought for their opinions." In the first few pages of *Walden* Thoreau set flattery between lying and voting.[25]

⤙ RULE 94: *Flattery isn't what it used to be.*

The Prince de Joinville, son of King Louis-Philippe, accompanied his father on a tour of France. In Bernay the king was advised that his party would be formally greeted by a series of addresses, including one from the local Président de Tribunal. The president advanced, made his bow with a prim look, and gave a very studied and impertinent lecture.

> Everybody listened in silence. It was all about courtiers, the danger of listening to flatterers, and so forth. As it ended, the heads of the president and his friends all came up with a "Take that, my fine fellow" look. . . . Then the King replied with the utmost politeness, thanking M. le Président for the advice he had been good enough to give him. "Flatterers and courtiers," he said, "have indeed done much mischief, and, sad to say, the race is not yet extinct, for nowadays there are courtiers who are far more dangerous than the flatterers of princes and of kings—those courtiers and flatterers of the people, who to buy a vain and contemptible popularity suggest to them dreams which are unrealizable and which bring them to misfortune."[26]

Touché, Your Highness.

Let us return to the most important flatteree: you again, dear reader. Doubly, triply, or infinitely souled, you will always be something of a mystery to yourself. No one is more surprised than you are by the things you say and do. A shallow narcissist would stop there, capitally flattered to be a Puzzle or a Paradox—or better, an Elemental Chaos or unwitting Tool of God. Self-flattery connives to blind you with an aureole. Ask yourself rather, how many yous are you? Don't be afraid to guess high. All by itself a conscience can be judge, accuser, defendant, and contradicting witnesses.

✤ RULE 95: *A skilled flatterer has many roles.*

After you identify how many yous you are, you better appreciate the You in charge. Love You as you ought to love. Kant, the cool skeptic, doubted that self-love was altogether bad, and saw that flattery benefits: "When we can bring any flattering thought of merit into our action, then the motive is already somewhat alloyed with self-love."[27] Having done the right thing, you are entitled to enjoy having done the right thing, and to enjoy compliments for doing so. Compliments may be all the reward there is—and scarce at that—yet be enough to induce desire for more. Rather than be satisfied by doing one thing right (the saving grace, the defining moment, the single skill), indulge the insatiable desire to do right again and again, for no greater reward than to be praised for it (Rule 39).

If no one else flatters your righteous You, you have a right to do it, as Stoics and saints did. Erasmus wrote: "Dicitur is rectè laudare sese, cui nemo alius contigit laudator"; Samuel Johnson translated this approvingly, "It is right that he, whom no one else will commend, should bestow commendations on himself." He adds, "Of all the sons of vanity, these are sure the happiest and greatest."[28]

6. Dangers

Power and superiority are so
flattering and delightful, that,
fraught with temptation,
and exposed to danger, as they
are, scarcely any virtue is so
cautious, or any prudence so
timorous, as to decline them.

SAMUEL JOHNSON

Ssu-ma Ch'ien (circa 145–85 BC), the first great historian of China, was castrated by an easily offended emperor but permitted to complete his *Shih chi*, an immense history of pre-Han China. Late in life, and late in the history, he allowed himself a complaint: "Today the rulers of men are sunk in the phrases of sycophants, caught in the coils of [those behind] curtains and skirts."[1] The complaint is worldwide. Tacitus's disgust of flattery erupts throughout his histories. The Talmud declares, "From the day the fist of flattery prevailed, justice became perverted."[2] Frederick the Great of Prussia remarked that there is no book of philosophy, no book of history, that does not condemn the fondness of weak rulers for flattery.[3]

With condemnations everywhere, why add more? When I review what fools some potentates were, I flatter myself that I could write a sharp and shocking chapter about flattery's mortal dangers, pages brimming with horror, blood-red pages denouncing flattery as a menace we must corner and kill. But it's been done, dear reader, and besides, you need no more frights or false alarms. You are not likely to repeat the blunders of snooty potentates. Still, you might be amused by them and in a few pages profit from what gave King Frederick so much trouble. I invite you now to amble down a wide and well-trodden path, observing flattery's debacles and disasters, with a pause now and then to do nature's duty. As a bonus, along the way you'll encounter the historical sources for charming tales you heard in childhood.

To speed us through thickets and revive a lively emblem, I'll frequently abbreviate "flatterer" to "fox."[4] Foxes flirt with danger, mix mischief with flattery and deceit with admonition. They make others wonder what the devil they'll do next. If they are sleek and independent, with no care about income or scandal, they devise tricks for the fun of it. But a hungry fox embarked up the social slope must take precautions and turn down temptations to taunt.

✦ RULE 96: *Flatterers are wary of irony.*

Irony is too easily mistaken for sarcasm. Well-made and well-delivered flattery begs to be understood. Though irony has the allure of appealing to intelligence (Rule 78), it is a gambit best reserved for secure relationships.

Flattery endangers high and low unequally. A fox chased into the open is torn to pieces, but history (that flatterer) prefers to dawdle on the dangers to potentates. For a fox dangers lie in misapprehension, mistiming, excess, envy, and cliché. For the potentate dangers lie in concealment and deception, in trumped-up fear and rivalry, in diversion from serious alarms, in somnolence, in addiction. For bystanders, danger lies in the embarrassment and disappointment that come from watching a potentate decay, or smelling a flatterer stink. For safety's sake, don't stand between a fox and its flatteree. "Meddle not with him that flattereth with his lips," warns the Proverb (20:19).

With a hyperbole that would be imitated ad nauseam, Tacitus declared that "flatterers are the worst kind of enemies."[5] An angry fox is a vengeful fox. A happy flatterer wants to keep the flatteree happy and well; a frustrated flatterer wants to humiliate and destroy. Saint Augustine admonished, "The dove loves when it quarrels; the wolf hates when it flatters."[6] He had imperial examples before him: Emperor Vitellius "concealed his hatred under servile flattery." Sapor, king of the Persians, "by carefully calculated flattery mingled with perjury" lured King Arsaces of Armenia to his death. Emperor Macrinus condemned Emperor Caracalla because he "took pleasure in flatterers, and approved as his loyal friends and supporters those who spurred him on to cruelty." Emperor Valens fell for "cruentis adulationibus" [bloodthirsty flatteries] and became savage.[7]

⤙ RULE 97: *Weak minds are dupes of flattery.*

Gaius Marius won over Gauda, "whose mind was weakened by ill-
ness, declaring he was a king, a mighty hero."[8] The praetorian prefect
Modestus tricked Valens, "who was somewhat simple-minded, with
veiled but clever flattery." He called the emperor's "rough, crude
words 'choice Ciceronian posies'; and to increase his vanity he declared that, if Valens should order it, even the stars could be brought
down and displayed for him."[9] Young James, Duke of Monmouth,
eventually king of England, had "a beautiful figure and engaging
manners. . . . it is no wonder that he was early assailed by the arts of
flattery; and it is rather a proof that he had not the strongest of all
minds, than of any extraordinary weakness of character, that he was
not proof against them."[10]

The innocent are endangered by flattery. King James's weakness
led to the revival of witch burning.

> The King, who was much celebrated for his knowledge, had, be-
> fore his arrival in England, not only examined in person a woman
> accused of witchcraft, but had given a very formal account of the
> practices and illusions of evil spirits, the compacts of witches, the
> ceremonies used by them, the manner of detecting them, and
> the justice of punishing them, in his Dialogues of *Daemonologie*,
> written in the Scottish dialect, and published at Edinburgh. This
> book was, soon after his accession, reprinted at London, and as
> the ready way to gain King James's favour was to flatter his specu-
> lations, the system of *Daemonologie* was immediately adopted by
> all who desired either to gain preferment or not to lose it. Thus
> the doctrine of witchcraft was very powerfully inculcated.[11]

The most dangerous flattery has been uttered many times and
many times believed, namely: *You can do whatever you want.* A
close student of kings, parliaments, and revolution, Edmund Burke
cited a classical example:

A king is ever surrounded by a crowd of infamous flatterers, who find their account in keeping him from the least light of reason, till all ideas of rectitude and justice are utterly erased from his mind. When Alexander had in his fury inhumanly butchered one of his best friends and bravest captains; on the return of reason he began to conceive an horror suitable to the guilt of such a murder. In this juncture his council came to his assistance. But what did his council? They found him out a philosopher who gave him comfort. And in what manner did this philosopher comfort him for the loss of such a man, and heal his conscience, flagrant with the smart of such a crime? You have the matter at length in Plutarch. He told him, "*that let a sovereign do what he wilt, all his actions are just and lawful, because they are his.*"[12]

Plutarch drew his authority from his vast study of history, from his praiseworthy character, and from his offices as Archon of Chaeronea and priest of Delphi. He saw firsthand that flattery "does not attend upon poor, obscure, or unimportant persons, but makes itself a stumbling-block and a pestilence in great houses and great affairs, and oftentimes overturns kingdoms and principalities." Richard Stengel adds that "Plutarch and the others never quite explained how flatterers overturn kingdoms and principalities," but for centuries historians have been busy recording instances.[13]

↬ RULE 98: *Flattery works like a drug.*

Often described as a poison, flattery soothes and anesthetizes (Rule 59). Or it stimulates. Insomniac Nietzsche warned, "People who want to flatter us to dull our caution in dealing with them are using a very dangerous tool, like a sleeping potion which, if it does not put us to sleep, keeps us only the more awake." When his foreign wars were not going well, Tiberius applied sycophancy as a distracting remedy.[14]

⤙ RULE 99: *Flattery is contagious.*

It spreads like disease. Shakespeare called flattery "the monarch's plague." Sir Richard Steele opened issue 238 of the *Spectator* with a health warning: "Among all the Diseases of the Mind there is not one more epidemical or more pernicious than the Love of Flattery." Recalling the state apparatus of Nazi Germany, Albert Speer warned, "There is a special trap for every holder of power, whether the director of a company, the head of a state, or the ruler of a dictatorship.

13. Flatterers in hell, Dante's *Inferno*, canto 18, by Gustave Doré (1861).

His favor is so desirable to his subordinates that they will sue for it by every means possible. Servility becomes endemic among his entourage, who compete among themselves in their show of devotion. This in turn exercises a sway upon the ruler, who becomes corrupted in his turn."[15]

Domitian had the usual faults of Roman emperors: greed, superstition, extravagance, cruelty. Cassius Dio grieved that Domitian "had this worst quality of all, that he desired to be flattered."[16]

↪ RULE 100: *Flattery breeds spite.*

Bad flatterers despise good flatterers, and vice versa, in a grinding wheel. Defoe wrote, "It is a very ancient observation, and a very true one, that People generally despise where they flatter, and cringe to those they design to betray." Hazlitt sneered: "Sycophants and flatterers are undesignedly treacherous and fickle. They are prone to admire inordinately at first, and not finding a constant supply of food for this kind of sickly appetite, take a distaste to the object of their idolatry. To be even with themselves for their credulity, they sharpen their wits to spy out faults, and are delighted to find that this answers better than their first employment."[17]

↪ RULE 101: *Flatterers mutate into informants and into agents of the police.*

Athenaeus wrote that Athens teemed with informers "when flattery, like a ravening beast, had injected its madness into the city."[18] In La Fontaine's "Funeral of a Lioness" a flatterer instantly becomes a spy. A kind of peak was reached by Anne Jean Marie René Savary, who became Napoleon's chief of secret police. "Prompt to perform the most criminal as well as the most the meanest offices—to be the executioner as well as the spy—and skillful to mix flattery with his bluntness, so as to render the former more acceptable, he was the slave of his employer, and of all slaves, the basest. He hesitated neither to superintend the murder of the Duke d'Enghien, nor to preside over the most odious system of espionage ever despot devised."[19] Savary glued loyalty to adulation, and rose higher and higher in Napoleon's circle, though everyone around him (let us not exclude Napoleon) knew what he was up to.

His affectation to extol everything that Bonaparte does, right or wrong, is at last become so habitual that it is naturalized, and you may mistake for sincerity that which is nothing but imposture or flattery. . . . [He] is now one of Bonaparte's adjutants-general, a colonel of the Gendarmes d'Elite, a general of brigade in the army, and a commander of the Legion of Honour; all these places he owes, not to valour or merit, but to abjectness, immorality, and servility. . . . He is so well known that the instant he enters a society silence follows, and he has the whole conversation to himself. This he is stupid enough to take for a compliment, or for a mark of respect, or an acknowledgment of his superior parts and intelligence, when, in fact, it is a direct reproach with which prudence arms itself against suspected or known dishonesty.[20]

Savary remained loyal, even going into exile with Napoleon, then outlived his emperor and served in the military of the restored monarchy. Flattery raised him to a position whence conspicuous obedience raised him higher still. His example tempers a frequently repeated rule:

❧ RULE 102: *Flatterers prevent rulers from hearing bad news.*

Saint-Simon wrote, "Princes and Monarchs who, by listening to those who flatter their pride and indolence, erect an insurmountable barrier against true information, and are thus led into irreparable errors."[21] Savary's case illustrates another rule:

⊶ RULE 103: *Flatterers take shelter in loyalty.*

A fox can be loyal or not, but in any case the appearance of loyalty is vital. A fox cannot shift allegiances quickly or often without being suspected by both the old and new flatteree. If a fox ditches a potentate in trouble, nothing could be more dangerous than for the potentate to return to power. Rather than bear such hazard, a wise fox would rather keep the friendly potentate safe and secure.

Aristotle, Plutarch, Philodemus, Cicero, and Maximus of Tyre were anxious to distinguish flatterers from friends.[22] Heap shame on the name of Scudilo, a tribune, who "under the cloak of a somewhat rough nature" mingled flattery with false oaths to lure Gallus to his death.[23]

⊶ RULE 104: *Humility flatters.*

Condescension is more difficult to hide than to express, but with practice it can look exactly like humility. Molière's Tartuffe and Dickens's Uriah Heep are literature's warning signals (Dickens's Carker in *Dombey and Son* is less known, but as bad as Heep). History has even more remarkable foxes, Julius Caesar its most notable. He "showed himself perfectly ready to serve and flatter everybody, even ordinary persons, and shrank from no speech or action in order to get possession of the objects for which he strove. He did not mind temporary grovelling when weighed against subsequent power, and he cringed as before superiors to the very men whom he was endeavouring to dominate."[24]

The complaint that flattery insulates too much is too universal to ignore. The most intimate friends of Vitellius, briefly Roman emperor in AD 69, kept unhappy truths from reaching him and "so inclined the emperor's ears that useful counsel sounded harsh, and he would hear nothing but what flattered." The duc de Saint-Simon blamed flatterers for Louis XIV's ruinous protracted wars.[25] Wounded, one leg amputated, and dying in fever, Marshal Lannes warned Napoleon, "Your ambition is insatiable, and will destroy you. You sacrifice unsparingly and unnecessarily those men who serve you best; and when they fall you do not regret them. You have around you only flatterers; I see no friend who dares to tell you the truth. You will be betrayed and abandoned." And what did Napoleon think? After conferring with Czar Alexander I, he condoled, "Sovereigns are most unfortunate, always deceived, always surrounded by flatterers or treacherous counselors, whose greatest desire is to prevent the truth from reaching the ears of their masters, who have so much interest in knowing it."[26]

History repeats the lesson again and again: potentates who should know better take bad advice from flattering attendants. Blaming flatterers for bad decisions is so recurring a danger that it has become a plausible excuse. John Motley, for instance, chides Robert Dudley, Earl of Leicester, because he "preferred to flatter his sovereign [Queen Elizabeth I], rather than to tell her unwelcome truths. More fortunate than Buckhurst, he was rewarded for his flattery by boundless affection, and promotion to the very highest post in England when the hour of England's greatest peril had arrived, while the truth-telling counsellor was consigned to imprisonment and disgrace."[27] Motley omits too much: as the queen's privy counselor, Leicester would not convey bad news unless absolutely necessary; instead, he would be expected to deal with it on his own authority. Further, as Motley knew, Leicester had hoped to marry Elizabeth, an ambition the queen turned to her own purposes. Though she entrusted him with commissions that his arrogance spoiled, he had political power of his own that she had to take into account. She knew a fox when she saw one, and he did her bidding after all.

Foxes in positions of power see their situations very differently from how bystanders see them. To a fox a potentate suffering from stress and danger needs all possible support to avoid panic or paralysis. On the other hand, maneuvering through the palace intrigues of France when it was ruled by Anne of Austria and Mazarin, Cardinal Retz put the matter as bluntly as anyone could: "There is nothing so dangerous as flattery at a juncture where he that is flattered is in fear, because the desire he has not to be terrified inclines him to believe anything that hinders him from applying any remedy to what he is afraid of."[28]

Two truths: (1) The truth is powerful; (2) "Some can tolerate the truth better than others."[29] Take the crowned examples—Tiberius, Elizabeth I, James I, Louis XIV, Napoleon—excepting the weak minded, potentates are more helped than harmed by flatterers' filtering out bad news. Bad news reached them readily enough, and usually they were capable of responding to it.

The propensity of potentates to be buffered from bad news has been sometimes overcome by means of a simple courtesy: a request for permission to tell the truth. As he prepared to invade Greece, Xerxes asked Demaratus, an exiled Spartan, whether the Greeks would dare to fight his enormous army. Demaratus took the precaution of asking, "O king, must I speak truly, or so as to please you?"[30]

⤙ RULE 105: *Flattery increases sensitivity to criticism.*

Racine told his son, "The applause I have met with has often flattered me a great deal; but the smallest critical censure, bad as it has always been, always caused me more vexation than all the pleasure given by praise."[31]

Other dangers are more serious. Flattery can make a potentate more famous than safe. Laurent Bordelon worried: "If they Praise me too much, they'll raise the Envy of other Men against me, and at the same time they'll excite their Curiosity; so that it'll be found that I am unworthy of the Praises that are bestowed upon me."[32]

↦ RULE 106: *Flattery corrupts.*

The unhappy reign of Charles I of England was made worse because King Charles believed his flatterers, and because others did, too. He took seriously their talk about "divine right" and "indiscriminate obedience."

> Men seemed to vie with each other who should have the honour of the greatest share in the glorious work of slavery, by securing to the king, for the present, and after him to the duke, absolute and uncontrollable power. They who, either because Charles had been called a forgiving prince by his flatterers (upon what ground I could never discover), or from some supposed connection between indolence and good nature, had deceived themselves into a hope that his tyranny would be of the milder sort, found themselves much disappointed in their expectations.
>
> The whole history of the remaining part of his reign exhibits an uninterrupted series of attacks upon the liberty, property, and lives of his subjects.[33]

Shakespeare described the problem:

> They do abuse the king that flatter him:
> For flattery is the bellows blows up sin;
> The thing which is flatter'd, but a spark.

Ben Jonson put it this way: "Flattery is midwife unto princes' rage."[34]

Flattery seldom harms the virtuous by itself, but when practiced in combination with the other devices of intrigue it can corrupt and ruin. Schiller describes the destruction of Thomas Armenteros, a man "up to this time of irreproachable character."

> By pretended professions of attachment and friendship a successful attempt was made to gain his confidence, and by luxurious entertainments to undermine his principles; the seductive example infected his morals, and new wants overcame his hitherto incor-

ruptible integrity. He was now blind to abuses in which he was an accomplice, and drew a veil over the crimes of others in order at the same time to cloak his own. With his knowledge the royal exchequer was robbed, and the objects of the government were defeated through a corrupt administration of its revenues. Meanwhile the regent wandered on in a fond dream of power and activity, which the flattery of the nobles artfully knew how to foster.[35]

This is the fully equipped flattery that worried Plato, flattery able to dress well, give grand dinners, cloud judgment with dreams, and pose as friendship.

A powerful flatteree surrounded by flatterers soon competes with some other flatteree surrounded by a similar coterie (Rule 40). Their competitions are sometimes genial and mutually stimulating and sometimes ruthless, limited solely by nature and imagination. When one would-be tyrant competes with another, religion, law, custom, ethics, and education might restrain but cannot stop cruelty, or stop praise for it.

↦ RULE 107: *Flatterers conspire to ruin rivals.*

Otho's counselors took "refuge in flattery to prevent anyone from daring to oppose their views." Burke watched colleagues "willingly conspire to flatter and aggrandize that authority from which they expect a confirmation of their own."[36]

↦ RULE 108: *When flatterees fight in factions, death soon comes.*

When Rome was young, Ferrex and his brother Porrex ruled jointly over Britain. "These two brethren continued for a time in good friendship and amitie, till at length through covetousnesse, and desire of greater dominion, provoked by flatterers, they fell at variance and discord." Historians dispute who killed whom, but agree one killed the other.[37] Procopius mentions Leon, "the prince of flatterers," whose power of persuasion turned Emperor Justinian's "crass stupidity to the destruction of his fellow-men."[38]

↬ RULE 109: *Flattery abets arrogance.*

An attentive witness to the imperial ambitions of the European powers, Edmund Burke saw how easy it was to persuade a potentate and a people to undertake a war of conquest. "We all are men; we all love to be told of the extent of our own power and our own faculties. If we love glory, we are jealous of partners, and afraid even of our own instruments. It is of all modes of flattery the most effectual, to be told that you can regulate the affairs of another kingdom better than its hereditary proprietors. It is formed to flatter the principle of conquest so natural to all men."[39]

↬ RULE 110: *Flattery abets avarice.*

Samuel Johnson wrote that "avarice is always poor" and that flattery made the wealthy want. "Every man, eminent for exuberance of fortune, is surrounded from morning to evening, and from evening to midnight, by flatterers, whose art of adulation consists in exciting artificial wants, and in proposing new schemes of profusion."[40]

Foxes take risks. If they flatter greater potentates, they face greater dangers. Megalomaniacs are infamously arbitrary, willing to slaughter a fox on a whim. The risks are substantial enough to tempt a savvy fox to stick to the modest, tacit, and true.

Failure is the first of all fox dangers. Flattering badly invites ridicule. "Philip of Macedonia, having been obliged to put on a Headband, because he was wounded in the Head," soon saw most of his courtiers wearing the same apparel.[41] The Abbé de Polignac is best remembered because he made a fool of himself. "One day when following the King through the gardens of Marly, it came on to rain.

The King considerately noticed the Abbé's dress, little calculated to keep off rain. 'It is no matter, Sire,' said de Polignac, 'the rain of Marly does not wet.' People laughed much at this, and these words were a standing reproach to the soft-spoken Abbé."[42]

Flatterers are found in more comedies than tragedies because of the fools some flatterers make of themselves. Cassius Dio warned that "every act of insincerity that one undertakes for the purpose of flattery is inevitably suspected."[43] Some foxes are caught. La Bruyère cites the example of a flatterer who "congratulated Theodemus on a Sermon which he had not heard, and which no body could give him any account of. He extoll'd his Genius, his Manner, and above all the Fidelity of his Memory, when in truth, Theodemus stopt in the middle of his Discourse, and forgot what he had designed to say."[44] Oops.

Failure can snap a string of successes if a fox encourages a potentate to aim too high.

↪ RULE 111: *Flattery endangers by overreaching.*

General Moreau, a celebrated and victorious commander, thought he could compete with Napoleon in politics, but "was destroyed" by flatterers who pushed him to strive too high.[45] In a famous case, Dionysius the Tyrant had enough.

> For when one of his flatterers, named Damocles, dilated in conversation upon his troops, his resources, the splendors of his despotism, the magnitude of his treasures, the stateliness of his palaces, and said that no one had ever been happier: "Would you then, Damocles," said he, "as this life of mine seems to you so delightful, like to have a taste of it yourself and make trial of my good fortune?" On his admitting his desire to do so Dionysius had him seated on a couch of gold covered with beautiful woven tapestries embroidered with magnificent designs, and had several

sideboards set out with richly chased gold and silver plate. Next a table was brought and chosen boys of rare beauty were ordered to take their places and wait upon him with eyes fixed attentively upon his motions. There were perfumes, garlands; incense was burnt; the tables were loaded with the choicest banquet: Damocles thought himself a lucky man. In the midst of all this display Dionysius had a gleaming sword, attached to a horse hair, let down from the ceiling in such a way that it hung over the neck of this happy man. And so he had no eye either for those beautiful attendants, or the richly wrought plate, nor did he reach out his hand to the table; presently the garlands slipped from their place of their own accord; at length he besought the tyrant to let him go, as by now he was sure he had no wish to be happy.[46]

Gibbon tucked the lesson into a figure, a feminine one: "Flattery is a foolish suicide; she destroys herself with her own hands."[47]

Canute the Great, king of England and greatest of the Viking lords, knew where to draw the line. A flatterer called him "king of kings," and Canute sought to reprove him. He went to the beach and ordered the tide to cease. "'Thou art (saith he) within the compasse of my dominion, and the ground whereon I sit is mine, and thou knowest that no wight dare disobeie my commandements; I therefore doo now command thee not to rise upon my ground, nor to presume to wet anie part of thy sovereigne lord and governour.' But the sea keeping hir course, rose still higher and higher, and overflowed not onelie the kings feet, but also flashed up unto his legs and knees."[48] Having made his point, Canute drove it home, telling his flatterers that only God is the King of Kings. He went to Westminster and set his crown upon the crucifix in the Church of Peter and Paul. If faith could not make Canute a humble Christian king, a Christian historian could.

Canute's episode would seem a clear case of natural law refuting flattery's propositions, but it teeters on a wire suspended between beliefs. Long before Canute, Callisthenes wrote that the sea *obeyed* Alexander the Great.[49] Xerxes whipped the sea when it did not obey him. In 1612, with religious strife still troubling England, a learned Jesuit, Robert Parsons, opposed the flattery of his Protestant adversaries who intoxicated Queen Elizabeth "with excessive praises, and immoderate adulations." To shame their weak faith and vile scheming he attacked with miracles: Saint Clement, who, when cast into the sea, saw the sea recede three miles to keep him safe, and Saint Gregory Thaumaturgus, who thrust his staff before a flooding river and stopped it from overflowing. Parsons believed that Protestants' scorn of miracles proved, as their flatteries proved, that they were damnable.[50]

⊕ RULE 112: *Tyrants crave flattery.*

Cruel rulers gulp praise. The flattery demanded by the succession of vain Roman emperors drove historians to despair whether honest history were possible. The most disastrous flatterer of the last century was Joseph Goebbels, Hitler's "most adoring disciple."[51] Goebbels initiated the "Heil Hitler" greeting, enforced the practice of deeming Hitler "der Führer," and devoted his life, talents, wife, and children to Hitler's glory.[52] As early as 1926 he wrote a letter to "Dear and revered Hitler," effusing, "I have learned so much from you! In your comradely fashion you have shown me fundamentally new ways which have finally made me see the light. . . . The day may come when everything will go to pieces, when the mob around you will foam and grumble and roar, 'Crucify him!' Then we shall stand firmly and unshakably and we will shout and sing 'Hosanna!'"[53]

✎ RULE 113: *Criminals are flattered by great crimes.*

Envy of the flattery of virtue feeds the voracious flattery of vice. To be the prince of thieves or mastermind of the massacre is to be flattered by victims and accomplices. Among champions listed in the *Guinness Book of World Records* is the most repetitious serial killer.[54]

Anesthesia, addiction, delusion, scorn, ridicule, brutality, hell. A field so full of dangers has brought forth heroes, strange as strange can be.

7. Heroism of Flattery

> Take those wild men
> sprung from rocks and
> trees — what power
> brought them together
> into a civilized society
> if not flattery?
>
> ERASMUS

In his *Phenomenology of Spirit* (1807) Hegel speculated about human progress. He supposed that sometime in the past "the heroism of silent service" became "the heroism of flattery [Heroismus der Schmeichelei]," a happy step forward marked by the appearance of kings. "The language of flattery raises this power into its purified *universality*. . . . it raises the individuality, which otherwise is only a presumed existence, into the existence of the pure form, by giving the monarch his own proper *name*." The monarch, "exclusive and solitary . . . knows himself, *this* individual, to be the universal power, knows that the nobles not only are ready and prepared for the service of the state power, but that they group themselves round the throne as an *ornamental setting*, and that they are continually telling him who sits on it what he *is*."[1] This is flattery in the form of philosophy, and it flatters philosophy honestly. Long before Hegel, philosophy flattered itself that it made kings and made them better. Plato taught Dionysius the Tyrant; Aristotle taught Alexander the Great.

Hegel's phrase "Heroes of flattery" looks ironic, an invitation to snicker and sneer. Written when Napoleon's cannon were blowing up a coalition of kings, Hegel's book did not assume any king was secure. The era of heroes of flattery could be passing away. It was a revolutionary insight, but he did not develop it. As it turned out the era was interrupted rather than over, and Hegel's restraint was rewarded. He became an immensely popular professor in Berlin, serving at the pleasure of a king. A prudent man, Hegel had written nothing to regret. Who were flattery's heroes? He named no names.

Hegel is seldom praised for his humor, but his "heroes of flattery" admit at least six types, five of them cheerful and one of them comic:

1. There are innumerable men and women who manage, through judicious flattery, to make love and raise children. Nothing is more heroic than that.

2. There are heroes who excelled in flattery: Alcibiades, Caesar, Cleopatra.[2]

3. There are potentates who, through patronage, manage to extract masterpieces from those obliged to flatter them: Augustus, Elizabeth I, Pope Julius II, Louis XIV.

4. There are heroes of flattery able to flatter in any situation. Aristippus is the prototype. Lord Russell thought Benjamin Disraeli was a flattery genius: "Once, sitting at dinner by the Princess of Wales, he was trying to cut a hard dinner-roll. The knife slipped and cut his finger, which the Princess, with her natural grace, instantly wrapped up in her handkerchief. The old gentleman gave a dramatic groan, and exclaimed, 'I asked for bread and they gave me a stone; but I had a Princess to bind my wounds.' "[3] Charles II received a flattering poem from Edmund Waller but complained that it wasn't as fine as a poem Waller composed for Cromwell. Waller replied, "Poets, Sir, succeed better in fiction than in truth."[4]

5. There are superheroes of flattery who raised flattery into high art: Michelangelo, La Fontaine, and Shakespeare. Shelley recalled that "Virgil was a flatterer."[5] Of the same type, though in a lesser league, are writers like Lucian of Samosata. His essay in praise of the fly is a textbook example of his ability to praise anything.

6. Most abundant are the men and women who imagine themselves heroes because somebody once flattered them. You know the type. They have become the common property of farce from here to anywhere.

 RULE 114: *Flattery can be fun.*

The fame of Louis XIV persists because of the splendor of his court and the artists he supported.[6] Superstitious, easily spooked, and nearly illiterate, King Louis loved flattery (Rule 112). "Praises, or to say truth, flattery, pleased him to such an extent, that the coarsest was well received, the vilest even better relished. It was the sole means by which you could approach him. Those whom he liked owed his affection for them to their untiring flatteries. This is what gave his ministers so much authority, and the opportunities they had for adulating him, of attributing everything to him, and of pretending to learn everything from him."[7]

As he grew old Louis XIV relied on strong women: first the Marquise de Montespan, then Mademoiselle de Maintenon. They were rumored to control him (Rule 16).

⤚ RULE 115: *People sensitive about their age are flattered by compliments about youthfulness.*

⤚ RULE 116: *Old men are flattered by the company of women.*

Louis respected the virtue of his wife, richly supported his mistresses until he tired of them, and sometimes raised their children. He "was flattered, even to idolatry."[8] His court was a flattery industry.

Louis entertained his favorites with newly commissioned plays by Corneille, Molière, and Racine. He let La Bruyère, La Fontaine, and La Rochefoucauld pass his censorship. All wrote about flattery; all practiced it. Complimented by the king for his genius, Molière responded, "Sire, my opinion is nothing compared to that which Your Majesty has just expressed, such is your sureness of judgment and your tact. I know by experience that those scenes of my comedies which, at a first reading, are applauded by Your Majesty, always win most applause from the public afterwards."[9]

La Fontaine portrayed Louis as Jupiter, king of the gods.[10] He was hardly alone. "The painters and sculptors, most artful of courtiers in their calling, had already represented the King, now with the attributes of Apollo, now in the costume of the god Mars, of Jupiter

14. "Allégorie à la gloire de Louis XIV," by Charles Le Brun (circa 1654).

Tonans, Neptune, lord of the waves; now with the formidable and vigorous appearance of the great Hercules, who strangled serpents even in his cradle."[11]

Reviewing the literary entourage of Louis XIV, François Guizot admires Racine, Boulieu, Madame de Sévigné, and especially Jean de La Bruyère, author of *Les caractères* (1688), "a book unique of its sort, full of sagacity, penetration and severity without bitterness."[12] In tone, decorum, and predilection, La Bruyère's book is a model for Guizot. I have often cited Guizot's *History of France* and should praise him a little. Like Plutarch and Tacitus, Guizot was a historian who knew politics from the inside; like them, he held high office in times of great political turmoil. He died while preparing his great *History of France*, begun for the sake of his grandchildren. The *His-*

tory was completed and published by his daughter, M. Guizot de Witt. My rebel heart clenches because Guizot was a rock-hard royalist, but that decision was made for him; his father was guillotined during the Terror.

Guizot praises *Les caractères* as a "picture of the manners of the court and of the world, traced by the hand of a spectator who had not essayed its temptations, but who guessed them and passed judgment on them all. . . . it was a brilliant, uncommon style, as varied as human nature, always elegant and pure, original and animated, rising sometimes to the height of the noblest thoughts, gay and grave, pointed and serious."[13] La Bruyère taught the court what it taught him about flattery. "We never look for happiness within ourselves, but in the opinions of men we know to be flatterers, insincere, unjust, envious, whimsical, and prejudiced. How eccentric!"[14]

↦ RULE 117: *Not everybody can know everything about flattery.*

In the next century came one of the greatest experts on flattery who ever duped a demagogue: Charles Maurice de Talleyrand-Périgord (1754–1838), bishop, ambassador, foreign minister, spy, conspirator, and counselor to kings. He was proud of what he knew and whom he knew (it is not whom you know, but what you know about whom you know that matters), even he did not know it all. "I am inclined to believe that flattery possesses secrets with which princes alone, — not those who have lost their thrones, but those who subjected their crowns to some ever-threatening protectorate — are acquainted; they know skillfully how to make use of them, when placed in the presence of the power which rules over and could overthrow them."[15]

Shuttling between potentates, Talleyrand watched flattery at work. "Everything magnifies, or rather swells, about a petty sovereign: etiquette, regard, and flattery; the latter is the standard of his greatness; he never thinks it is exaggerated."[16] In a world ruled by royalty, who were flattery's elite? And who now?

From the dawn of religion in Egypt and Babylon to the great faiths of the modern world, union with God has been a cherished goal. Poor people seeking God have been comforted that priests and prophets and suffering and sacrifice will bring God closer. As if called by heaven, potentates are predisposed to believe that God works through them.

↦ RULE 118: *When religion enters politics it arouses supernatural flattery.*

In imperial Rome and imperial China, rulers claimed divine appointment or divine descent. Hernán Cortés conquered Mexico by claiming to be a resurrected god. Assessing the merits of the Reformation, Henry VIII made himself head of the Church of England and seized its property. Napoleon reopened the churches of France, but kept the pope captive at Fontainebleau.

↦ RULE 119: *Deification is flattery's highest form.*

Where power is worshipped (and where is it not?) deification of rulers is a seductive political goal. Heroes and rulers were thought to attain divinity, to achieve *apotheosis*, whereby they became able to heal, protect, advise, and otherwise answer prayers. Thebes deified Hercules. Mytilene deified Theophanes.[17] Rome deified routinely.[18] Japan deified Hirohito. Rastafarians worship Haile Selassie, the late emperor of Ethiopia.

An account is preserved of Alexander the Great discussing religious policy with his retinue. According to Arrian (circa AD 150), the story was widely known among Greeks and Romans. Anaxarchus, a philosopher, calculated the advantages of proclaiming Alexander a god:

It would be far more just to reckon Alexander a god than Dionysus and Heracles, not so much because of the magnitude and nature of Alexander's achievements but also because Dionysus was a Theban, and had no connection with Macedon, and Heracles an Argive, also unconnected with Macedon, except for Alexander's family, for he was descended from Heracles; but that Macedonians in their turn would be more justified in paying the respect of divine honours to their own king; in any case there was no doubt that when Alexander had departed from men they would honour him as a god; how much more just, then, that they should give him his due in life rather than when he was dead and the honour would profit him nothing.

The Macedonians who had been with Alexander throughout his campaigns were uneasy. One of them, Callisthenes, then stood up and disagreed. "Among the gods themselves all are not honored in

15. Apotheosis of Antoninus Pius and Faustina (second century AD). The imperial couple rides an angel.

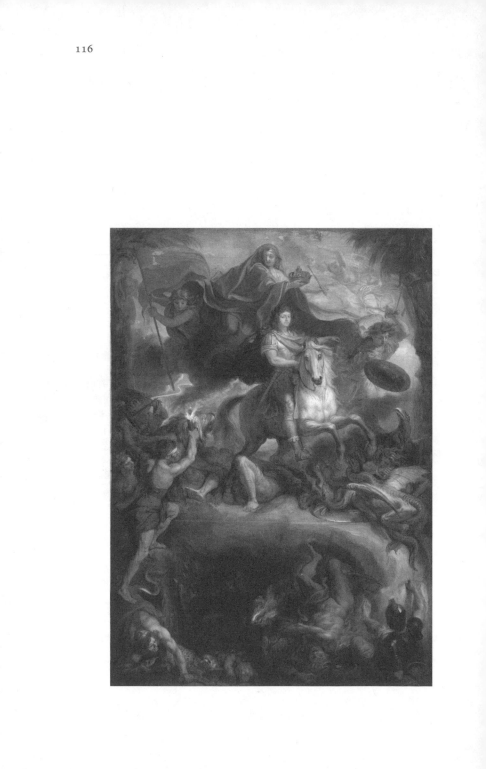

16. "Apotheosis of Louis XIV," by Charles Le Brun (1677). Louis XIV (1638–1715) was very much alive when this was painted.

17. "The Apotheosis of Napoleon," by Ingres (1853). Napoleon died in 1821.

18. "Apotheosis of Washington,"
by John James Barralet (1802).
Washington died in 1799.

the same way; and what is more, there are different honours for the heroes, distinct again from those paid to gods. It is not, therefore, proper to confuse all this, by raising mortals to extravagant proportions by excesses of honour, while bringing the gods, as far as men can, down to a demeaning and unfitting level by honouring them in the same manner as men."[19] Alexander was persuaded otherwise and allowed himself to be honored as a god.[20]

Athens deified Demetrius Poliorcetes in 307 BC, and he responded by setting up house in the Parthenon. "The Athenians overreached themselves in their flattery, when they offered to Marcus Antonius their goddess Athena as a bride. The Roman accepted the honour, but to the consternation of the Athenians he demanded of them the right royal dowry of one thousand talents and exacted mercilessly the payment of the sum."[21]

In the stormy years of Rome's transition from a republic to an empire, Cicero wrote *De Natura Deorum*, his great book on theology. Citing Hercules, Aesculapius, and Romulus as examples, he wrote that human experience and general custom "have made it a practice to confer the deification of renown and gratitude upon distinguished benefactors."[22] Soon deification would be a Roman habit.

The senate of Rome voted to declare that Julius Caesar and Caesar Augustus were gods, but neither waited for a vote. Julius Caesar set up his own cult with temples, altars, and priest. Augustus "left small room for the worship of heaven, when he claimed to be himself adored in temples and in the image of godhead by flamens and by priests!"[23]

More than belated praise for the impotent departed, deification had consequences that made Roman republicans deeply suspicious of rulers in bed with religion. The words of deified Augustus were retroactively divine. His views on law were upheld because he held them. To doubt the divinity of a deified Caesar risked arraignment for sacrilege and treason. The proliferation of new gods became a public nuisance; temples required priests, and priests required incomes; cults competed for favor and sued each other in court; petty criminals hid behind effigies of deified Caesars to claim sanctuary.[24]

Until it became ordinary, deification offered high praise to a deceased Caesar and held his successors to high standards. The Caesars who followed Augustus wished to be treated like gods, too, but discovered that comparisons with Augustus, if not mere flattery, could lead to unflattering distinctions. The Augustan Age became the eternal ideal of the status quo, providing precedent for Caesars' absolute power and arguments for rebellion against unworthy Caesars.[25]

Tiberius foresaw the pitfalls of routine deification. He allowed eleven cities of Asia to compete in raising a temple to him, then regretted it, seeing an ominous trend.

> Since the deified Augustus had not forbidden the construction of a temple at Pergamum to himself and the City of Rome, observing as I do his every action and word as law, I followed the precedent already sealed by his approval, with all the more readiness that with worship of myself was associated veneration of the senate. But, though once to have accepted may be pardonable, yet to be consecrated in the image of deity through all the provinces would be vanity and arrogance, and the honour paid to Augustus will soon be a mockery, if it is vulgarized by promiscuous experiments in flattery.[26]

But the precedent and its temptations were too enticing and useful. Caligula deified his sister Drusilla.[27] Claudius deified Livia, wife of Augustus, and was himself deified.[28] Nero deified his dead infant daughter and his wife, Poppaea, whom he killed with a kick.[29] Domitian demanded to be addressed as "Dominus et deus noster" [our Master and our God], a practice later revived "by one emperor after another."[30] Hadrian deified Trajan and his lover Antinous and raised temples to himself. Antoninus Pius deified Hadrian and was himself deified.[31] Marcus Aurelius, Commodus, Pertinax, Septimius, Severus, Severus Alexander, Aurelius Claudius, and Aurelian were

deified. Elagabulus dressed up as the Great Mother and as Dionysus.[32] When Hölderlin, Nietzsche, and Nijinksy claimed to be gods,
they were dismissed as madmen; when heads of state dress in piety,
pay the priesthood, and echo scripture, they are revered.

Caligula began "to lay claim to divine majesty" and gave orders
that "such statues of the gods as were especially famous for their
sanctity or their artistic merit, including that of Jupiter at Olympia,
should be brought from Greece, in order to remove their heads and
put his own in their place."[33] Caligula's insistence on having his own
statue placed in the Temple of Jerusalem ignited the Jewish rebellion. Lucius Vitellius obliged Caligula's pretensions: "He had also a
wonderful gift for flattery and was the first to begin to worship Gaius
Caligula as a god; for on his return from Syria he did not presume
to approach the emperor except with veiled head, turning himself
about and then prostrating himself."[34] Vitellius later became Caesar
himself, holding the throne for eight months till slain in civil war.

Caracalla murdered his brother Geta and covered up the crime by
having him deified.[35] Macrinus assassinated Caracalla and resorted
to the same expedient.[36]

Caligula a god, Commodus a god, Elagabulus a god—what could
people think of religion with gods like these? Appian of Alexandria,
a historian of Rome's civil wars, pondered the paradox: the Romans
called Caesars gods at death though "they could not bear to call
them kings while living."[37]

A lightning-bright counterexample occurred in Judea in the reign
of Claudius. King Herod Agrippa entered the theater at Caesarea
dressed all in silver.

> Straightaway his flatterers raised their voices from various di-
> rections—though hardly for his good—addressing him as a god.
> ... The king did not rebuke them nor did he reject their flattery
> as impious. But shortly thereafter he looked up and saw an owl
> perched on a rope over his head. At once, recognizing this as a

harbinger of woes just as it had once been of good tidings, he felt a stab of pain in his heart. He was also gripped in his stomach by an ache that he felt everywhere at once and that was intense from the start. Leaping up he said to his friends: "I, a god in your eyes, am now bidden to lay down my life, for fate brings immediate refutation of the lying words lately addressed to me." . . . Even as he was speaking these words, he was overcome by more intense pain.[38]

After suffering five days he died.

✦ RULE 120: *Potentates who wish to be praised as gods do so at their own risk.*

Looking to their rulers, people everywhere have imitated them. The potent symbolism of a ruler as a god or representative of a god permits poor souls to surrender to credulity and suppose that obedience makes them holy. Empires have been built on such faiths and destroyed by them. If monsters like Caligula and Commodus could be deified, deification should be possible for anyone. The great proselytizing religions promise nothing less.

Apostolic fathers of the early Christian church were quick to denounce the pretense of Caesars in favor of the faithful. In the second century Justin Martyr declared, "We have learned that those only are deified who have lived near to God in holiness and virtue." A little later Tertullian wrote, "The name of piety is more grateful than the name of power; the heads of families are called fathers rather than lords. Far less should the emperor have the name of God." For a Caesar to claim to be God is a "most unworthy, nay a fatal flattery."[39] Great martyrs declared that they could not pray to Caesars, but they could pray for them.[40] The opinion was rendered obsolete after the conversion of Constantine in AD 337. Thereafter Christian bishops addressed Christian Caesars as *divus*: "divine Constantine," "divine Theodosius," "divine Arcadius."

As Jesus himself is said to have done (John 10:34–36), early Christian theologians pondered Psalm 82:6 — "You are gods; and all are sons of the Most High."[41] Clement of Alexandria (circa AD 153–220) advised that "the Word of God became man, that thou mayest learn from man how man may become God." In the late fourth century, Saint Gregory of Nazianzus declared, "I might be made God as far as He is made Man."[42] Through much of Christendom, there is no higher ambition than to be wholly a part of God.

What a thought — to be God, altogether one. It is a wish enormous and attractive, delightful to imagine, and rapturous to believe. Tribonian flattered Emperor Justinian by saying he was "quite terrified that sooner or later as a reward for his piety the Emperor would be carried up to heaven and vanish from men's sight."[43]

People work all week to be with God for an hour or so. The great faiths support divinity schools that train professionals to be with God full-time. Since people know people pretty well, people tend to give credit to God when prayers are answered and blame themselves when they are not. Since people tend to know their own limits, they turn to saints, priests, and pastors for help in improving the power of prayer. The step into prayer, void of superstition, is a step into the infinite, and wherever flattery has room to expand, it will.

8. To Flatter God

A true and noble theology
can hardly fail to recognise,
in the love of Nature and
care for our fellow-men thus
promoted, something far
better, both from a religious
and a moral point of view,
than any efforts to win the
Divine favour by flattery.

ANDREW DICKSON WHITE

Alone with his thoughts and the universe, twenty-two-year-old Benjamin Franklin wrote down his religious credo in "Articles of Belief and Acts of Religion" (1728):[1]

> When I stretch my Imagination thro' and beyond our System of Planets, beyond the visible fix'd Stars themselves, into that Space that is every Way infinite, and conceive it fill'd with Suns like ours, each with a Chorus of Worlds for ever moving round him, then this little Ball on which we move, seems, even in my narrow Imagination, to be almost Nothing, and my self less than nothing, and of no sort of Consequence.
>
> When I think thus, I imagine it great Vanity in me to suppose, that the *Supremely Perfect*, does in the least regard such an inconsiderable Nothing as Man. More especially, since it is impossible for me to have any positive clear Idea of that which is infinite and incomprehensible, I cannot conceive otherwise, than that He, *the Infinite Father*, expects or requires no Worship or Praise from us, but that he is even INFINITELY ABOVE IT.

Though Franklin saw the idea was a "great Vanity," he observed in "all Men a natural Principle which enclines them to DEVOTION or the Worship of some unseen Power."[1] From this he concluded that he, too, should worship.

Two points stand out: Franklin asserts that religious devotion is (1) natural; and (2) universal. Whatever his doubts, nature and natural principles demanded his acquiescence, an attitude that allied him with a host of scientists, philosophers, and clergy who sought to fortify religion with the precise study of nature.

Franklin went on: "It seems required of me, and my Duty, as a

Man, to pay Divine Regards to SOMETHING," namely, to the "Author and Owner of our System," whom he proposed as the "Object of my Praise and Adoration" and whom he loved for his goodness and adored for his wisdom. "Let me then not fail to praise my God continually, for it is his Due, and it is all I can return for his many Favours and great Goodness to me."[2] Franklin withheld allegiance to a church or sect, preferring to roam at large within the universal. From stars above and an urge within he concurred with the great religions that it is a duty, a universal duty, to praise God.

Whether God is Baptist, Catholic, Muslim, Hindu, Jewish, or Jehovah's Witness, holy scriptures testify that God, who needs nothing, wants praise, lots of it, and often. The first sūra of the *Koran* declares, "Praise be to God." The *Rig Veda* commands, "Sing praise to him, the Lord of Light." The *Bhagavad Gītā* instructs, "It is wholly just that in praise of You the world should find its pleasure and its joy."[3]

⤙ RULE 121: *God must be praised.*

It was for his praise that the Holy One brought the Hebrews out of Egypt. Moses said, "The Lord has recognized you this day as his special possession, as he promised you, and to keep his commandments; he will raise you high above all the nations which he has made, to bring him praise and fame and glory, and to be a people holy to the Lord your God, according to his promise" (Deuteronomy 26:18–19). God told Isaiah, "I have formed this people for myself and they shall proclaim my praises" (Isaiah 43.21). God told Jeremiah, "I bound all Israel and all Judah to myself, so that they should become my people to win a name for me, and praise and glory" (Jeremiah 13:11). The psalmist commands everyone: "All you kingdoms of the world, sing praises to God" (Psalms 68:32).

King David assigned "four thousand to praise the Lord on the musical instruments which David had made for the service of praise" (1 Chronicles 23:5). As prelude to a great ceremonial sacrifice of seventy bulls, a hundred rams, and two hundred lambs, "King Hezekiah and his officers commanded the Levites to praise the Lord in the words of David and of Asaph the seer. So they praised him most joyfully" (2 Chronicles 29:30). Belief is not enough, sacrifice is not enough. In his deep mystery, God demands to be praised with his powers and glories. The psalmist sings, "We owe thee praise, O God," and promises to "bless the Lord continually; his praise shall be always on my lips" (Psalms 65:1, 34:1). Nature itself praises God. Psalm 148 bids birds and beasts, mountains and hills, angels and stars to join in the praise of God.[4] Praise is the duty of the universe.

Where praise goes, flattery follows. In nations and communities that consider public expressions of piety to be mandatory, a hypocrite needs no rewards from heaven to make hypocrisy worthwhile. Plato complained, "In these days of ours, when . . . some men have no belief in gods, others hold that they give themselves no concern about us, and the creed of the worst, who are the majority, is that if they pay their gods a trifle in the way of sacrifice and flattery, they will lend their help in vast frauds and deliver the sinner from all sorts of penalties."[5]

↪ RULE 122: *Hypocrites praise God lavishly.*

Flattery enters into religion through doors, screens, and stained-glass windows, wherever people expect admiration for how well they praise. Crafty Reynard preaches to geese on the stained glass of Ely Cathedral and the Kirby Wharfe Parish Church and in carved pulpits all across England.[6] Thick and persistent flattery infiltrates religion through a favorite route: self-flattery. Good people with willing hearts have been known to suppose God is with them when they pursue incredibly dumb decisions. God, they say, knows better than they or we do. When decisions turn to ashes and mud, self-flatterers readily rely on God as an excuse.

↬ RULE 123: *The dangers of flattery magnify when they merge with the dangers of religion.*

In religion, self-flattery completely fools itself into thinking itself supreme (all rules apply, especially Rules 2, 8, 14, 19, 22, 65, 78, and 85). Amid innumerable praises to God, some are flatteries, and some of these flatter the flatterers, proud of their praises. In the middle of a hymn to Shiva, the seven sages say, "Honored by you, we think highly of ourselves."[7] Who would not be honored to be called upon by God, to be the summoned servant, or one of a choir, enraptured to the highest joy by joining in heavenly praise? A man like Franklin would appreciate the energy of such ambition.

"The melting-pot is for silver and the crucible for gold, but praise is the test of character," says Proverbs 27.21. Praise tests the character of the person praising and the character of the person praised; when more than memorized muttering, praises test relationships. What can be professed? What should be implicit? What should be discreet? What can be believed? If praise of God is the most important praise, it ought not to be mindless and hackneyed, yet there are risks and fears when departing from formulas. It is acceptably humble to repeat hosannas written by those whose natural inclinations to praise were better gifted with grace. It is also a dodge and a laziness: repetitive praise numbs. Kant thought people are prone, "when their hearts are disposed to religion, to transform what really has reference solely to their own moral improvement into a courtly service, wherein the humiliation and glorifications usually are the less felt in a moral way the more volubly they are expressed."[8]

To cease praising God with the same old praise, poets, painters, sculptors, composers, glaziers, athletes, builders, and architects prepare their praises with labor, love, and diligence. At minimum flattery is practice for praise (Rule 33), and practice for the praise of God is taught devoutly. Pay for praise has produced masterpieces: chants, anthems, masses, and magnificats, portraits painted in the

Sistine Chapel, the chapel itself, temples, shrines, basilicas, mosques, cathedrals, and pagodas.

In heaven are pleasures we vaguely imagine, bliss beyond understanding. But if heaven is what the person seeks, praise is flattery, since reward is desired most selfishly. The praising person seeks not just anything, but what is most precious, and praises for it. Even if the person is modest and seeks nothing more than the pleasure of praising God (a pleasure saints expressed as ecstasy), still a reward is wanted, and the praise passes the first rule of flattery.

The hearty spontaneous praise of God expressed at births, rescues, and starry nights, the cantatas and masses of Handel and Bach, the thumping hearts that pray their blood will say what words cannot, are praises that rise unburdened by ulterior motives. Congregations that gather to praise God in the faith that praise is due, and who believe their duty is to give it, escape flattery's sullied reputation. But as soon as the taint of expectation enters praise, the instant the soul asks for something in return—health, wealth, victory—so soon do the dangers of flattery intrude.

Legend has it that Satan's rebellion began when he ceased to flatter God. Satan said, "I can be a God, as well as He. . . . It seems not right to me that I need flatter God any whit for any benefit; no longer will I be His follower."[9]

↭ RULE 124: *Flattery is as old as Eden.*

Satan promised Adam and Eve that they would be as gods; to be as God is the eldest temptation. It worms into religions' wonderful promises: freedom from hurt, freedom from evil, freedom from death. To feel such freedom would be to be like God, and that is possible, some say, if people ask God's help to become so. How ask without succumbing to the old temptation?

Peasants hated haughty priests who claimed to be closer to God in order to be closer to potentates. Lord Halifax observed: "There is a Right Reverend Flattery that hath the Precedence of all other Kinds of it. This Mitred Flattery is of others the most exalted. It ever growth in proportion, and keepeth pace with Power."[10]

Can God be flattered? Perhaps not, but people have been caught trying. Psalms recite the wanderings of the Exodus and the waywardness of the emancipated Hebrews. "They did flatter Him with their mouth, and they lied unto Him with their tongues" (Psalm 78:36). In the third century AD, Tertullian complained that people who stress God's mercy and ignore his justice "flatter God and pander to themselves."[11] Succeeding centuries, with their crusades, pogroms, torture, and slavery, cannot be accused of stressing mercy too much.

⊷ RULE 125: *Vainglory is most flattered when it thinks it thinks like God.*

With heavenly justice as assured as heaven itself, conquerors leave their victims to God's mercy and give them none of their own.

⊷ RULE 126: *A reputation for religion is flattering.*

Who but God could count the crimes committed in God's name? People and nations flatter themselves by calling themselves holy, proudly showing religious insignia on flags, lapels, and the paraphernalia of politics. They easily believe they're religious because they flatter each other that they are (Rule 31).

19. Two scenes in one woodcut from *Reynke de Vos* (1498). In the foreground Reynard affects holiness, and in the background he seizes the gullible Cock.

20. Pious Reynard, by Wilhelm von Kaulbach (1846). The iconography of pious foxes tricking pious birds goes back at least to the fourteenth century.

But this is trite. Praises from the megaphone have their place, even if abused sometimes. The flattery that slips into the praise of God goes much deeper: literally, physically, to the heart of the matter: the human heart.[12] Human hearts imagine the heart of God. A popular American hymn sings:

> There is a place of quiet rest,
> near to the heart of God;
> a place where sin cannot molest,
> near to the heart of God.[13]

Theophilus of Antioch wrote that "the Word, that always exists" resides in "the heart of God."[14] That God's heart is immaterial is immaterial: what matters is that his heart feels sympathy, yearning, and love, like our hearts. Our hearts help us understand God as nothing else can, except perhaps our minds.

Our minds imagine the mind of God. Marcus Aurelius wrote to himself: "It would assist thee greatly if thou bear the Gods in mind and that it is not flattery they crave but for all rational things to be conform'd to their likeness."[15] Aurelius was a pagan and an emperor, what could he know? This much, at least: that God was not merely within reason, but was reason's purpose, and that God wanted rational souls to be as rational as he is. That is much to expect, much to ask.

It is a commonplace that common folk imagine God like themselves. The second commandment prohibits images of God, but the Torah impresses us that we should wonder what is meant by God's face, his back, his hands, his feet, his sight, his hearing, and his voice. Despite the commandment, Christian artists have fearlessly depicted God as a powerful man with long white hair, an image previously projected on Zeus and Jupiter and more recently imitated by poets, singers, and imams.

Alarmed that Christianity had succumbed to idol worship, Emperor Leo III began a war against images in 726. Against stiff opposition he commanded that all religious images be destroyed. Statues, paintings, embroidered altar cloths, and mosaics of the Virgin, the Christ child, saints, evangelists, and prophets were abhorred, hacked to pieces, burned, buried, or covered in plaster.[16] Saint Germanus defied the emperor and pointed to scripture: Saint Paul presented Christ as "the image of the invisible God," the "express image of his person" (Colossians 1:15 and Hebrews 1:3).[17] Christians offended by Leo's prohibition rose in revolt. "They armed a fleet of boats and gallies, displayed their consecrated banners, and boldly steered for the harbour of Constantinople, to place on the throne a new favourite of God and the people."[18] They prayed for God's aid in overthrowing the emperor, but God gave Leo the victory. The images felt Leo's righteous wrath. He took too seriously a simple rule:

↣ RULE 127: *Anthropomorphic images of God flatter people.*

Leo trusted his gut, enforced a commandment, and incited rebellion; as Gibbon neatly put it, he "held it to be the duty of a prince, to impose on his subjects the dictates of his own conscience."[19] Leo died; the resistance did not. In 843 iconophile Empress Theodora restored images to veneration. Praise and worship triumphed over commandment and law, hagiography triumphed over history. Legalization brought image industries back to life, enriching commerce and reinforcing credos. Icons thrive today, and are up to date. Jesus has been depicted skiing, jogging, and buffed up in boxing shorts.[20]

Sensitive souls are scandalized by such images. When able to leave the law courts and public business, free to think about heavenly things, Cicero scorned the presumption of human gods.

> Was there ever any student so blind as not to see that human shape has been thus assigned to the gods either by the deliberate contrivance of philosophers, the better to enable them to turn the hearts of the ignorant from vicious practices to the observance of religion,

or by superstition, to supply images for men to worship in the belief that in so doing they had direct access to the divine presence?
These notions moreover have been fostered by poets, painters and
artificers, who found it difficult to represent living and active dei-
ties in the likeness of any other shape than that of man.[21]

For Cicero, a human God is a fiction, but a useful one. Useful, and
thus susceptible to misuse. Cicero added: "Nothing is more difficult than to divert the eye of the mind from following the practice
of bodily sight. This difficulty has caused both uneducated people
generally and those philosophers who resemble the uneducated to
be unable to conceive of the immortal gods without setting before
themselves the forms of men: a shallow mode of thought."[22]

Christianity sometimes lost its balance trying to determine how
God as man is to be understood. Heresies sprang up that tipped
too far one way or another: the Socinians thought that Jesus was
completely human, and the Sabellians thought he only appeared
that way. Franklin avoided the issue: missing from his "Articles of
Belief" is any mention of Christ, or any hint of interest in gods who
became men, like Vishnu, or of men who began religions, like Bud-
dha.[23] Franklin praised and thanked God the Creator for Creation:
Franklin is plain patriotic proof that an intelligent man can endure
the fact that he is a particle in an immense universe, can admit he
will be atomized, will return to celestial dust, and nonetheless praise
God.

In 1841 Ludwig Feuerbach's *The Essence of Christianity* analyzed
how much modern Christianity sanctifies the human body, human affections, human relationships. Feuerbach declared that "the
true sense of Theology is Anthropology," that "Christianity, while
lowering God into man, made man into God."[24] Feuerbach didn't
miss much: Christian ideas of man as God and God as man inform
doctrines about Creation, the personal God, Eucharist, incarnation,
God the father, and Mary the mother of God. An almighty God who

made man in his image, who made laws for humanity, who cares for nations and individuals and intervenes in their behalf, who demands human praise, pities human suffering, who was born, suffered, and died for humanity, is a God who loves humanness. Feuerbach quotes Saint Augustine: "Deus homo factus est, ut homo Deus fieret" [God made himself human that he might make man divine].[25]

Feuerbach saw how human traits were implicated in human images of God, and how flattering the images are. Confidence in God's forgiving love, more certain than a parent's love, tended toward arrogance. "Faith gives man a peculiar sense of his own dignity and importance. The believer finds himself distinguished above other men, exalted above the natural man; he knows himself to be a person of distinction, in the possession of peculiar privileges; believers are aristocrats, unbelievers plebeians."[26]

Like Socrates and Kant, Feuerbach found God in goodness. "The conception of the morally perfect being is no merely theoretical, inert conception, but a practical one, calling me to action, to imitation, throwing me into strife, into disunion with myself; for while it proclaims to me what I ought to be, it also tells me to my face, without any flattery, what I am not."[27]

Like Pythagoras, Marcus Aurelius, and Newton, Feuerbach found God in reason: "Of God as God no image can be made. . . . God as God — as a purely thinkable being, an object of the intellect — is thus nothing else than the reason in its utmost intensification become objective to itself."[28]

Like Paul, Vatsyayana, and Lucretius, Feuerbach found God through love. "God as God has not saved us, but Love, which transcends the difference between the divine and human personality."[29]

Feuerbach was surprised that his book was widely read — he had written it for philosophers and theologians — but he took its notoriety in stride. In 1843 he published a second edition, then a third. He declared:

God is love: that is, feeling is the God of man, nay, God absolutely, the Absolute Being. God is the nature of human feeling, unlimited human feeling, made objective. God is the optative of the human heart transformed into the *tempus finitum*, the certain, blissful "is,"—the unrestricted omnipotence of feeling, prayer hearing itself, feeling perceiving itself, the echo of our cry of anguish. . . . In prayer, man addresses God with the word of intimate affection—*Thou*; he thus declares articulately that God is his *alter ego*; he confesses to God, as the being nearest to him, his most secret thoughts, his deepest wishes, which otherwise he shrinks from uttering. . . . Prayer is the absolute relation of the human heart to itself, to its own nature; in prayer, man forgets that there exists a limit to his wishes, and is happy in this forgetfulness.[30]

Here Feuerbach is forgetful and upstart. He neglects troubled prayers painfully aware of their limits, prayers of perpetual falling, prayers of despair. He admits that prayer can fool and indulge itself but forgets that prayer sometimes is pure waiting, pure anticipation. He is upstart because he supposes that "man forgets," but he does not. But Feuerbach is on the side of the saints in stressing that prayer requires concentration and that concentration requires forgetfulness. In nature he sees that "prayer is the absolute relation of the human heart to itself." That is not all it is.

Prayer, too, has rules. In prayer one must speak honestly about oneself, humble oneself, repent oneself, in order to open oneself to God or God's messenger. Feuerbach criticized his contemporaries who worshipped their personal God "in the undoubting certainty that their personal, self-flattering wishes will be fulfilled, i.e., in the certainty of the divine nature of their emotions, the truth and unassailableness of their subjective feelings."[31]

✑ RULE 128: *The means and ends of prayer make it a paradise for flattery.*

Biblical prayers entwine petition and praise. "About midnight Paul and Silas, at their prayers, were singing praises to God" (Acts 16.25). The third chapter of *Tobit* begins with a prayer, and the prayer begins with praise: "O Lord, thou art just, and all thy works and all thy ways are mercy and truth, and thou judgest truly and justly for ever. Remember me, and look on me; punish me not for my sins and ignorances, and the sins of my fathers, who have sinned before thee." Then, as if correcting an error, Tobit asks for exactly the opposite: "Deal with me according to my sins and my fathers' . . . deal with me as seemeth best to thee." Tobit then asks to die.

Typically prayers begin with praise and pass into petition. Hallowed art Thou, now give me this and that. With God as an audience—God is always listening—a speaker need not speak to be heard. God knows all. Then why pray? Why try to put in words what the heart says silently and what God already knows? The call to prayer concedes that the heart cannot get God's love just by needing it; the heart must ask. Instruction in prayer, first by rote, then by scrupulous attention, concedes that prayer must be practiced. Prayer demands the repression of selfishness and pretension, yet what could be more selfish than this: to think that the Creator of the universe cares to hear and will stop to listen? Franklin could scarcely believe it. Feuerbach supposed Christians believed they reached God every time they prayed. He forgets the terror of prayer—that the prayer might fail, that maybe God will not heed.

What can a person pray for? Saint Paul's contemporary Apollonius of Tyana made it plain and simple: "It appears to me that a person who comes to the house of God and has a good conscience, should put up the following prayer: 'O ye gods, grant unto me that which I deserve.'"[32] Yet prayer is seldom plain and simple. Hearts yearn, questions choke, weary souls fumble for the right words and seek guidance to get them right. Praise is a good way to start, defining the difference between mortal desire and almighty omniscience.

In the Gospel of Matthew Jesus instructs his disciples about the proper way to pray: privately. "When you pray, go into your room, shut the door, and pray to your Father in secret" (6:6–14).[33] He then provides a model, the Lord's Prayer, which begins with praise, and which long ago left privacy to be recited by enormous congregations.[34] A conversation with God, private as private can be, may be less effective than an assembly trained in prayer, but it is less prone to hypocrisy or hypnotism, more particular, more intimate, and more certain of its motives and needs. Private, personal prayer goes its own way, and its praises test character.

To assess the quality of prayer by results (Rule 10) would observe that God has answered prayers of many religions. The dead and deified pagan emperor Julian was credited with answering prayers.[35] Pagan though he was, Marcus Aurelius was reputed to have had God's ear. "By his prayers he summoned a thunderbolt from heaven against a war-engine of the enemy, and successfully besought rain for his men when they were suffering from thirst."[36] A coincidence maybe, but it was an event so impressive that Xiphilinius, a Christian historian, in his commentary on the event, gave credit for the rain to the prayers of Christian soldiers.[37]

To flatter God truly, telling nothing but the truth, does not assume a fox can fool him (Rule 68). It behooves the praying fox to be honest and upright (Rule 9) and to respect God's intelligence (Rule 78). If the flattery is to succeed, it must please (Rule 2), and it does not please God to ignore unhappy facts: despite the earnest prayers of the faithful, children die, disasters strike, and armies massacre. The lord of a massacre flatters himself that he has done God's will (Rule 113).

The Talmud, to its glory, records its high-minded disputes about catastrophe. Rabbis debated whether remembrance of disasters might sow doubt about the love and power of God. They decided the truth must be told: "They knew that God valued truth and thus they would not flatter God falsely."[38]

9. Farewell

> Even in the very warmest,
> friendliest, and simplest
> relations, flattery or
> praise is needed just as
> grease is needed to
> keep wheels going round.
>
> **LEO TOLSTOY**

We come to the end of our climb up the hills with foxes. In recompense for your company, I leave you three gifts:

First, souvenirs of Paris and Rome.
Second, adulation for your impressive reading skills.
Third, best wishes for your future. If you like, we might
    meet again by a Sphinx or a campfire.

If you find something to take from this book, take also my thanks. All I ask in return is that you lovingly flatter your family and friends. Buy fresh new copies of *In Praise of Flattery* for them and inscribe compliments all your own.

ACKNOWLEDGMENTS

This book benefited from the encouragement and advice of dear friends and my beloved brother Phil. Finished in the spectacular library of the University of Illinois, it began twenty years ago in the kitchen of Warren and Marie Motte. Warren and I were discussing flattery in academia and he proposed I write a book about it. I've been taking notes ever since.

William Kohlhaase was newly in love and did not like to be distracted, but he denied himself, not too bitterly, and read through the first complete draft.

William Kinderman, a fox, wanted more pages on Fox, but I demurred. Fox has already been well described and illustrated in Kenneth Varty's *Reynard, Renart, Reinaert*, a book I heartily recommend. Though I do not cite Varty much, every page of my book admires every page of his. I admire William Kinderman for at least eighty-eight reasons, and this book has gained from his sense of humor and knowledge of music. He and his wife, Katherine Syer, talked me back from several speculative chasms.

At a crucial point, when my drafts and notes were moldering in a heap, Jeanne Weinkle raised my spirits and told me to get on with it.

The books and conversations of Avital Ronell have pioneered scholarship that zings, shouts, and laughs out loud. As I finished this, she finished her *ÜberReader. In Praise of Flattery* is proud to praise her.

Amy Howland McDavid, *ma très chère amie*, kept me from taking myself too seriously. Parts of this book are written for her.

Plutarch's high regard for friendship has been burnished for decades by Dr. Julia Lauer-Chéenne and Dr. Dominique Chéenne.

They have opened their hearts to my whimpers and their pantry to my appetite.

Rex Wallace coaxed and coached me through many a language seminar. He and Maureen Ryan made me unafraid of Roman tyrants and Greek panegyrists.

When I'd grown weary of this work Laurie Obbink persuaded me it still might be fresh to others. That's so like her, refreshing things!

Tom Eakman, Larry Mann, Sylvia Manning, and Chet Gardner have been my bosses while I wrote *In Praise of Flattery*. They're too wise to accept compliments at face value, knowing better than I do how flatterers inveigle and beguile, but because they are praiseworthy I praise them here and now as highly enlightened potentates.

Other potentates whose good opinion I desire include librarians, professors of history and languages, lawyers, judges, long-lost lovers, governors, musicians, publishers, painters, poker players, bookstore managers, and reviewers.

I thank my editor, Ladette Randolph, for her faith in this project, and Sandra Johnson, who helped me decide that the time had come to complete it.

My copyeditor, Robin DuBlanc, flattered me with her questions and corrections (Rule 78 holds no mysteries for her) and made this a better book.

A mighty potentate indeed is William Germano, dean of Liberal Arts at Cooper Union. He and his wife, Diane Gibbon, will read this book scrupulously, reason enough to earn floods of thanks.

Same to you, dear reader. All honor to you.

NOTES

PREFACE

1. Goethe, *Autobiography*, 69.

2. Stengel, *(You're Too Kind)*, 33.

3. "¡Oh fuerza de la adulación, cuánto te extiendes y cuán dilatados limites son los de tu juridición agradable!" Cervantes, *Don Quixote* (part 2, chap. 18), apropos the knight's mad praise for the poetry of Don Lorenzo.

4. Hume, letter to Gibbon, March 18, 1776, quoted in Gibbon's *Autobiography*, 177.

5. Athenaeus, *Deipnosophists*, 6.234c–262a.

6. Plato, *Phaedrus*, 240b, in *Collected Dialogues*, 487.

7. Tacitus, *Histories*, 1.15.

8. Doris, *Secret Memoirs of Napoleon*, 1:54–57. Doris published the memoirs anonymously. They blend fact, rumor, and invention. Pharamond (c. 370–c. 430) was the first king of the Salian Franks.

9. As an example to all self-flatterers, Balzac "wrote a very flattering article on his own work in *La Caricature*, over one of his three pseudonyms," Keim and Lumet, *Honoré de Balzac*, 112.

1. WELCOME

Epigraph: "Fortuna cum blanditur captatum venit," Publilius Syrus, *Sententiae*, §277. Also, Ben Jonson: "Who would trust slippery chance? . . . They that would make / Themselves her spoil; and foolishly forget, / When she doth flatter, that she comes to prey," *Sejanus*, 5.729–32.

1. "There being three principall things, without which all praising is but Courtship and Flattery, First, when that only is prais'd which is solidly worth praise: next when greatest likelihoods are brought that such things are truly and really in those persons to whom they are ascrib'd, the other, when he who praises, by shewing that such his actuall perswasion is of whom he writes, can demonstrate that he flatters not," Milton, *Areopagitica*, 487.

2. "The man who is pleasant in the proper manner is friendly, and the observance of the mean is friendliness; he that exceeds, if from no interested motive, is obsequious, if for his own advantage, a flatterer," Aristotle, *Nicomachean Ethics*, 2.7.13.

3. L'Estrange, *Fables*, 67; Johnson: "We every day see men of eminence followed with all the obsequiousness of dependance, and courted with all the blandishments of flattery, by those who want nothing from them but professions of regard, and who think themselves liberally rewarded by a bow, a smile, or an embrace," *The Rambler*, no. 166, October 19, 1751, 5:119.

4. Hazlitt, "On Will Making," in *Table Talk*, 118.

5. Plutarch, "How to Tell a Flatterer from a Friend," 275, 277.

6. Mandeville, *Fable of the Bees*, 1:42–43. Colton summarized Mandeville: "All the virtues are nothing more than the political offspring that flattery begets upon pride," *Lacon*, 440.

7. Burke, "A Philosophical Inquiry into the Origin of Our Ideas of the Sublime and Beautiful," in *Works*, 1:122.

8. Quoted by Madame de Montespan, *Secret and Historic Memoirs*, 2:171.

9. Bowen, "Art of Flattery," 121.

10. Colton, *Lacon*, 127. In the first edition the maxim is numbered CCX-VII. Henry James trimmed it to "Imitation is the sincerest flattery," *Portrait of a Lady*, chap. 19. A slight misquote, "Imitation is the sincerest form of flattery," is ubiquitous. Plutarch describes at length how a flatterer imitates the flatteree, "How to Tell a Flatterer from a Friend," 281–98.

11. In London, *Lacon* went through fourteen editions in two years. Editions were published in New York by Peter Burtsell (1821), Kingsland (1821), E. Bliss and E. White (1822 and 1823), S. Marks (1824), J. Montgomery (1824), S. King (1825), C. P. Fessenden (1832), Charles Wells (1832 and 1836), E. Kearny (1836 and 1840), and William Gowans (1849, 1855, 1860, and 1866); in Philadelphia by A. Sherman (1824) and by Porter & Coates (1849 and 1871); in Concord, New Hampshire, by Isaac Hill (1828); and in Utica, New York, by H. Gray (1823) for Thomas Longworth in Savannah.

12. Colton, *Lacon*, 127. Jean-Jacques Rousseau used the same flattery in *Emile*: "It is not easy for a man to begin to think; but when once he has begun he will never leave off. Once a thinker, always a thinker," 217. More flattering is Feuerbach's idealism: "To think is to be God," *Essence of Christianity*, 40.

13. Colton, *Lacon*, 15, 9. Colton committed suicide in 1832.

14. Colton, *Lacon*, 59.

15. Holmes, *Professor*, 255.

16. Aristotle, *Nicomachean Ethics*, 10.3.11.

17. "Vitiorum adiutrix," Cicero, "De Amicitia," §24; "Filthy science," Fulwell, *Ars Adulandi*, 85 and passim; "worst of vices," Harflete, *Hunting of the Fox*, 6; "prostitution of empty praise," Blackwell, *Memoirs*, 1:199.

18. Thomas à Kempis, *Christian's Pattern*, book 1, chap. 8.

19. Adams, *Writings*, 2:273.

20. For Greek synonyms see Ribbeck, *Kolax*, 93–100.

21. Masson, *Secret Memoirs*, 2:40.

22. Constant, *Recollections*, 1:131–32. Alcides refers to Hercules, grandson of Alceus.

23. The rebuke of Racine (quoted by Guizot in his *History of France*, 4:402) echoes the opening line of the *Mémoires* of Marguerite de Valois, addressing Abbé Brantôme, "Je louerais advantage votre oeuvre, si elle ne me louait tant"; Lucian, "The Way to Write History," in *Works*, 2:115.

24. Gibbon complained that the "science of form and flattery" was reduced "into a pompous and trifling volume" in Constantine Porphyrogenitus's *De Ceremoniis aulae Byzantinae*, which formalized the titles appropriate to different sovereigns and functionaries, *Decline and Fall*, 3:399.

25. In her study of African praise poems, Judith Gleason remarks that "an African thinks of himself as having not one but several souls. This plurality . . . confounded the misguided missionaries who had gone out to save just one soul per person," *Leaf and Bone*, 54. In "Song of Myself" Walt Whitman sang, "I am large . . . . I contain multitudes."

26. "The frequent and familiar companions of the great, are those parasites, who practice the most useful of arts, the art of flattery," Gibbon, *Decline and Fall*, 2:179 (chap. 31). This "art" is part of Gibbon's irony. In the same passage he jibes the "sublime science" of backgammon.

27. Meredith, *The Egoist*, 308.

28. Machiavelli, *The Prince*, 78.

29. Saint-Simon, *Memoirs*, 1:343–44.

30. Athenaeus, *Deipnosophists*, 6.237d–e. For other classical precedents see Ribbeck, *Kolax*, 32–42, 61–70. Plutarch secured the simile· "Vermin depart from dying persons and forsake their bodies, as the blood, from which the vermin derive their sustenance, loses its vitality; and so flatterers are never so much as to be seen coming near where succulence and warmth are lacking, but where renown and power attend," "How to Tell a Flatterer from a Friend," 267–69.

31. Huxley, *Point Counter Point*, 210–11; Emerson, "Power," in *Conduct*

of Life, 975; Nietzsche, "On Old and New Tablets," *Also Sprach Zarathustra*, 3.12.19, in *Portable Nietzsche*, 320; Shaw, *Revolutionist's Handbook*, 736.

32. Colton, *Lacon*, 210.

33. Burke, "A Philosophical Inquiry into the Origin of Our Ideas of the Sublime and Beautiful," in *Works*, 1:124.

34. Reuth, *Goebbels*, 176, 180, 200.

35. Doris, *Secret Memoirs of Napoleon*, 2:67–68.

2. FLATTER YOURSELF

Epigraph: Plutarch, "How to Tell a Flatterer from a Friend," 265.

1. Washington, "Circular Letter to State Governments," June 8, 1783, in *Writings*, 518; Madison, *Federalist*, #41, in *Writings*, 230; Hamilton, *Federalist*, #34, #66, #75, in *Writings*, 310, 353, 403; Franklin, *Writings*, 1421. Stengel discusses Franklin's self-promotion in detail, *(You're Too Kind)*, 170–76.

2. Bacon, "Of Friendship," in *Moral and Historical Works*, 78. Also, "the arch-flatterer, which is a man's self," "Of Praise," in *Moral and Historical Works*, 141.

3. Chesterfield, *Letters to His Son*, 1:28.

4. "It is necessary to the success of flattery, that it be accommodated to particular circumstances or characters, and enter the heart on that side where the passions stand ready to receive it. A lady seldom listens with attention to any praise but that of her beauty; a merchant always expects to hear of his influence at the bank, his importance on the exchange, the height of his credit, and the extent of his traffick: and the author will scarcely be pleased without lamentations of the neglect of learning, the conspiracies against genius, and the slow progress of merit, or some praises of the magnanimity of those who encounter poverty and contempt in the cause of knowledge, and trust for the reward of their labours to the judgment and gratitude of posterity," Johnson, *The Rambler*, no. 106, March 23, 1751, 4:199–200.

5. Chesterfield, *Letters to His Son*, 1:28; Stengel, *(You're Too Kind)*, 155.

6. Shawn Colvin's *Whole New You* (Sony Records, 2001) assures You you have the right.

7. Halifax, *Complete Works*, 240. "La vertu n'irait pas si loin si la vanité ne lui tenait compagnie," La Rochefoucauld, *Maximes*, 50; *Maxims*, 70.

8. Excepting only "retainer to His Majesty," these are the titles he listed himself at the head of his will; La Rochefoucauld, *Maximes*, xi, note 1.

9. Maxim #2: "L'amour-propre est le plus grand de tous les flatteurs," La Rochefoucauld, *Maximes*, 7; *Maxims*, 33.

10. La Rochefoucauld, *Maximes*, 134–35; *Maxims*, 140.

11. Maxim #123: "On n'aurait guère de plaisir si on ne se flattait jamais," La Rochefoucauld, *Maximes*, 33; *Maxims*, 55.

12. Maxim #144: "On n'aime point à louer, et on ne loue jamais personne sans intérêt. La louange est une flatterie habile, cache, et delicate, qui satisfait différemment celui, qui la donne, et celui qui la reçoit. L'un la prend comme une recompense de son mérite; l'autre la donne pour faire remarquer son équité et son discernement," La Rochefoucauld, *Maximes*, 38; *Maxims*, 59.

13. Maxim #425: "La pénétration a un air de deviner qui flatte plus notre vanité que toutes les autres qualities de l'esprit," La Rochefoucauld, *Maximes*, 98; *Maxims*, 111.

14. Burke mentions a flatterer who told Cardinal Mazarin that the wedding of young Louis XIV and Princess Marie-Thérèse of Spain "had removed mountains . . . the Pyrenees were levelled by that marriage," "Fourth Letter on the Proposals for Peace" [1795–97], in *Works*, 6:20.

15. Shelley, "On the Punishment of Death," in *Essays and Letters*, 67.

16. Kammen, *Mystic Chords of Memory*, 626.

17. Huxley, *Grey Eminence*, 101; Talleyrand, *Memoirs*, 5:340.

18. Plutarch, "Pericles," §14, in *Lives*, 3:47. For Tacitus, see *Histories*, 1.1.

19. Crabbe, "Birth of Flattery," 194.

20. "Ko 'tibhārah samarthānām kim duram vyavasāyinām / Ko videshah suvidyānāhah parvah priyavādinām," Hertel, *The Panchatantra*, 29. Ryder's translation alludes to Terence's famous line "Homo sum: humani nihil a me alienum puto," *Heautontimorumenos*.

21. *The Most Delectable History of Reynard the Fox*, 13–14.

22. "Si nous ne nous flattions point nous-mêmes, la flatterie des autres ne nous pourrait nuire," "Quand les vices nous quittent, nous nous flattons de la créance que c'est nous qui les quittons," La Rochefoucauld, *Maximes*, 40, 49; *Maxims*, 61, 68.

23. The trio consulted together and published separately: the duc and Madame published *Maxims* and Esprit published *La fausseté des vertus humaines*. Jacques Truchat, introduction to La Rochefoucauld, *Maximes*, xviii.

24. Taine, *The French Revolution*, 2:35.

25. Maxim #231: "C'est une grande folie de vouloir être sage tout seul," La Rochefoucauld, *Maximes*, 59; *Maxims*, 76.

3. WHY FLATTER?

Epigraph: Taine, *The French Revolution*, 2:1.

1. L'Estrange, *Fables*, 399; Wright, *Gentleman's Miscellany*, 134; Balzac, "The Reproach," 178–79.

2. Erasmus, *Praise of Folly*, §44.

3. Nietzsche, *Human, All Too Human*, §250.

4. Stengel, *(You're Too Kind)*, 255.

5. Quoted by Isaacson, *Kissinger*, 148. Isaacson's excellent index leads to startling examples of Kissinger's fawning.

6. Macaulay, "Machiavelli," in *Critical and Historical Essays*, 2:23–24.

7. Quintus Cicero (or a pseudo-Cicero) wrote that flattery is "etenim cum deteriorem aliquem adsentando facit, tum improba est, cum amicorem, non tam vituperanda" [vile when used to corrupt someone, but less despicable when used to reconcile friends], *Commentariolum Petitionis*, §42.

8. Shakespeare, *Henry V*, 3.7.110.

9. Plutarch, "How to Tell a Flatterer from a Friend," 275; Lamb, February 13, 1797, in *Complete Works and Letters*, 620.

10. Tolstoy, *War and Peace*, 397.

11. Plutarch, "Alcibiades," §24, in *Lives*, 4:67; Plutarch describes Alcibiades' flatteries in "How to Tell a Flatterer from a Friend," 283–85; on Martius Verus, see Cassius Dio, *Roman History*, 71.3.1.

12. Maxim #150: "Le désir de mériter les louanges qu'on nous donne fortifie notre vertu; et celles que l'on donne à l'esprit, à la valeur, et à la beauté contribuent à les augmenter," La Rochefoucauld, *Maximes*, 39; *Maxims*, 60.

13. Shakespeare, *Two Gentlemen of Verona*, 2.4.147.

14. Pliny, "Sed sane blandiantur, dum per hoc mendacium nobis studia nostra commendent," *Letters*, 1.2; Tolstoy, *Resurrection*, 546; Surtees, *The Analysis of the Hunting Field*, 10.

15. Kautilya, *Arthashastra*, 713.

16. Tacitus, *Annals*, 4.74.

17. Tacitus, *Histories*, 1.85; Isaacson, *Kissinger*, 279.

18. Plutarch, "Crassus," §6, in *Lives*, 3:331; Motley, *History of the United Netherlands*, 2:233, 2:139.

19. Maxim #152: "Si nous ne nous flattions point nous-mêmes, la flatterie des autres ne nous pourrait nuire," La Rochefoucauld, *Maximes*, 40; *Maxims*, 61.

20. Bordelon, *Management of the Tongue*, 85.

21. Chesterfield, March 16, 1752, in *Letters to His Son*, 2:75.

22. Colton, *Lacon*, 210; Shakespeare, *Julius Caesar*, 2.1.207; Jonson, Epigram #35, in *Poems*, 19; Flaubert, *Dictionary of Accepted Ideas*, 39.

23. Burr, letter to Matthias Ogden, June 18, 1776, in *Memoirs*, 1:82.

4. HOW TO FLATTER

Epigraph: Hume, *Treatise of Human Nature*, 348.

1. Aesop, *Fables*, 53; Phaedrus, *Fables*, 1.13; Babrius, *Fables*, 77; Marie de France, *Fables*, 62–65; La Fontaine, *Fables* 1.2; and many others; for Greek versions, see Chambry, *Aesopi Fabulae*, 2:285–87; Perry, *Aesopica*, #124. Joseph Jacobs traces the fable back to Buddhist *Jātakas*, in which a crow and jackal flatter each other, *History of the Aesopic Fable*, 65–66. For other flattering foxes, Jacobs draws attention to Berachyah ha Nakdan's medieval Jewish fable collection *Meshle Shu'alim* [Fox Fables] and Eremia's medieval Armenian collection *Agho-Vesarik* [The Fox Book], 176–77.

2. Translations of the fable often substitute Crow for Raven, though the Greeks knew the difference. Aesop has a fable about Crow pretending to be Raven and fooling no one, *Fables*, 153.

3. "Apprenez que tout flatteur / Vit aux dépens de celui qui l'écoute: / Cette leçon vaut bien un fromage, sans doute," La Fontaine, *Fables* 1.2, *Oeuvres complètes*, 1:32.

4. Rousseau, *Emile*, 77–81. Louis Marin presses the lesson at length in *Portrait of the King*, 94–104.

5. "Fox and Crow" is analyzed in Fulwell's *Ars Adulandi*, 114–16; Harflete's *Hunting of the Fox*, 45–46; L'Estrange's "Reflection," in *Fables*, 67–68; and Croxall's "Application," in *Fables*, 13–14.

6. Rousseau, *Emile*, 207; 159.

7. Emerson, "Swedenborg," in *Representative Men*, 661.

8. Kierkegaard, Nietzsche, and Paul de Man invite us to judge philosophers by their seductions.

9. Plutarch, "How to Tell a Flatterer from a Friend," 327. Plutarch elsewhere attributes this to Pittacus, "Dinner of the Seven Wise Men," in *Moralia*, 2:353. The phrase gained fame in English through Ben Jonson: "Of all wild beasts, preserve me from a tyrant, / And of all tame, a flatterer," *Sejanus*, 1.437–38. Diogenes Laertius reports that when asked what creature's bite is the worst, Diogenes the Cynic replied, "Of those that are wild a sycophant's; of those that are tame, a flatterer's," *Lives*, 6.51. Alexander Pope added, "It is the Slaver kills, and not the Bite," "Epistle to Dr. Arbuthnot," 104–6.

10. Athenaeus, *Deipnosophists*, 6.254c. Diogenes Laertius attributes this expression to Antisthenes, *Lives*, 6.4.

11. Diogenes Laertius, *Lives*, 6.92.

12. Only fragments remain; see Glad, "Frank Speech, Flattery, and Friendship," 22–23.

13. Diogenes Laertius, *Lives*, 2.66; 2.79.

14. Plato, *Gorgias*, 500b–503, in *Collected Dialogues*, 283–86.

15. Smith, *The Turkey*, 61.

16. Plutarch, "Phocion," §8, in *Lives*, 8:161, 163.

17. Plutarch, "Alexander," §23, in *Lives*, 7:189, 291.

18. Dryden, *Works of Virgil*, xv.

19. Lichtheim, *Ancient Egyptian Literature*, 1:198.

20. Howarth, "Puzzle of Flattery," 123, 133.

21. Schlegel, *Lectures*, 410.

22. Stewarton, *Secret Memoirs*, 2:48–49, 2:161–62.

23. Scott, "The Lay of the Last Minstrel," 4.35.33–34; Guizot, *History of France*, 3:129.

24. Johnson, *Lives*, 2:113.

25. Johnson, *Lives*, 2:97.

26. Sidney, *Astrophil and Stella*, §106. Shakespeare, *Richard II*, 2.2.68–72. Simrock, "An den Mond," "nur ein schmeichlerisches Hoffen / sei's, das sie zusammenhält," *Gedichte*, 10; Brahms repeats the lines in his setting of the poem (Opus 71, No. 2).

27. Bordelon, *Management of the Tongue*, 85.

28. Bordelon, *Management of the Tongue*, 88, 91.

29. Bordelon, *Management of the Tongue*, 89.

30. Bordelon, *Management of the Tongue*, 92.

31. Bordelon, *Management of the Tongue*, 93. Plutarch counseled that "the most shameful way of disavowing the name of flatterer is to cause pain without profit; and it shows an utterly rude and tactless disregard of goodwill," "How to Tell a Flatterer from a Friend," 353.

32. The *Manual* was first published in London in 1652. Its author was not a Spanish minister, but the book is a translation of Eustache du Refuge's *Traicté de la cour* (1615?). Walsingham was supposed to be the true author and the "Spanish Minister" a pretense typical of the period. A later English edition appeared as *Arcana Aulica; or, Walsingham's Manual of Prudential Maxims* (London: M. Gillyflower, 1694). This was translated back into French as *Le secret des cours, ou les mémoires de Walsingham, secrétaire d'état sous la reine Élisabeth* (1695), mistaking Edward Walsingham for Francis Walsingham, Elizabeth's head of espionage.

33. Walsingham, *Manual*, 130.

34. Quoted in Adams, *History of the United States*, 278–79.

35. Ssu-ma Ch'ien, *The Grand Scribe's Records*, 7:182.

36. Shestov, *All Things Are Possible*, 32.

37. Bourrienne, *Memoirs*, 2:50.

38. Adams, *Writings*, 3:256.

39. In Aristophanes' *The Knights*, Demos confides, "I love to drink the lifelong day, and so it pleases me to keep a thief for my minister. When he has thoroughly gorged himself, then I overthrow and crush him," *Eleven Comedies*, 1:65.

40. Doris, *Secret Memoirs of Napoleon*, 1:100. Doris quotes this opinion then disagrees with it, saying Napoleon would have been a tyrant as a schoolmaster, king, or corporal of the guard.

41. Méneval, *Memoirs*, 1:134–36.

42. Méneval, *Memoirs*, 1:145.

43. Talleyand, *Memoirs*, 1:314.

44. Méneval, *Memoirs*, 2:608.

45. Talleyrand, *Memoirs*, 1:315. Bourrienne reported that Talleyrand "was almost the only one among the ministers who did not flatter Bonaparte," *Memoirs*, 2:182.

46. Macaulay, *History of England*, 1:131, on Charles I.

47. Geoffrey of Monmouth, *History of the Kings of Britain*, 233.

48. Hobbes, *Leviathan*, 74.

49. Johnson, *The Rambler*, no. 155, September 10, 1751, 5:61. Beethoven, "Die Welt ist ein König, / u. sie will geschmeichelt seyn, Soll sie sich günstig zeigen — / Doch wahre Kunst ist/eigensinnig, läßt sich nicht in Schmeichelnde/Formen zwängen," *Ludwig van Beethovens Konversationshefte*, Hefte 9, c. March 11–19, 1820, 1:326.

50. Emerson, "Gifts," 535.

51. For Mademoiselle d'Aumale, see Montespan, *Secret and Historic Memoirs*, 1:99; for Mademoiselle de Fontanges, see Monstespan, *Secret and Historic Memoirs*, 2:90–97.

52. Nietzsche, *Human, All Too Human*, §574.

53. Russell, *Collections and Recollections*, 223, 224. Disraeli learned the lesson from experience; he borrowed the trowel from Lord Halifax, who wrote in 1750, "Generally speaking, a Trowel is a more effectual Instrument than a Pencil for Flattery," Halifax, *Complete Works*, 251. Carlyle noted that Voltaire flattered Frederick the Great with a "strongish trowelful, thrown

on direct, with adroitness," and gave two examples from 1740: Voltaire told the king that the *Anti-Machiavel* "is a monument for the latest posterity; the only Book worthy of a King for these Fifteen hundred years," and "I put more value on this Book than on the Emperor Julian's *Cæsar*, or on the *Maxims of Marcus Aurelius*," Carlyle, *History of Friedrich II*, 4:42. Also Shakespeare, "Well said; that was laid on with a trowel," *As You Like It*, 1.2.96.

54. Nietzsche, *Twilight of the Idols*, "Skirmishes of an Untimely Man," §11 in *Portable Nietzsche*, 521.

55. Montespan, *Secret and Historic Memoirs*, 1:26–32.

56. Plutarch, "Publicola," §10, in *Lives*, 1:527.

57. Cassius Dio, *Roman History*, 57.18, and Suetonius, "Tiberius" §26, in *Lives of the Caesars*.

58. When Nero refused the honor he was still under the restraint of Seneca, his tutor. Tacitus, *Annals*, 13.10, 16.12.

59. *Scriptores Historiae Augustae*, 1:125, 1:293; Cassius Dio, *Roman History*, 73.15. See also Beurlier, *Culte impérial*, 46–47.

60. Plutarch, "Numa," §1, in *Lives*, 1:307; Gibbon, *Decline and Fall*, 1:177, and *Autobiography*, 80.

61. Kooser, *Poetry Home Repair Manual*, 3–4.

62. "The Seductress," in Vermes, *Dead Sea Scrolls*, 395.

63. Pliny, *Letters*, 2.14; Cassius Dio, *Roman History*, 62.20.

64. *Tso chuan*, 111.

65. Loyseau, *Treatise*, 123.

66. Le Roy Ladurie, *Saint-Simon*, 4.

67. La Fayette, *Memoirs*, 168–69.

68. Stewarton, *Secret Memoirs*, 156–58.

69. Croxall, *Fables*, 14.

5. THE FLATTEREE

Epigraph: Jonson, *Timber*, §84.

1. *Government of the Tongue*, 148.

2. Aristotle, *Nicomachean Ethics*, 8.8.1.

3. Bowen, "Art of Flattery," 134.

4. Gibbon, *Decline and Fall*, 2:640.

5. Tolstoy, *War and Peace*, 1053. For Tiberius, see Tacitus, *Annals*, 2.87 and Suetonius, "Tiberius," §27, in *Lives of the Caesars*; for Galba, Tacitus, *Histories*, 1.35; for Marcus Aurelius, *Meditations*, 1.16. For Severus Alexander, see *Scriptores Historiae Augustae*, 2:211.

6. Bismarck, *The Man and the Statesman*, 2:313.

7. Le Sage, *Gil Blas*, 183; book 4, chap. 7.

8. Spinoza, *Ethics*, 2:240.

9. "It is the Parasite's Art to cast himself into all Shapes that may sort with the Figure of his Patron," L'Estrange, *Fables*, 68.

10. *The New English Bible* reads, "good news warms a man's marrow."

11. Shakespeare, *Timon of Athens*, 1.1.226.

12. Philaenis, *Perì aphrodisíon*, now known only through fragments; see Marcovich, "How to Flatter Women."

13. "Plato admits four sorts of flattery, but she had a thousand," Plutarch, "Antony," in *Lives*, 9:201.

14. Tocqueville, *Democracy in America*, 171. For more on Tocqueville, see Stengel, *(You're Too Kind)*, 182–88.

15. Le Roy Ladurie, *Saint-Simon*, 14.

16. Bowen, "Art of Flattery," 133.

17. Fay, *Shostakovich*, 175–76.

18. Juvenal, "nihil est quod credere de se non possit, cum laudatur dis aequa potestas," *Satires*, 4.70–71.

19. Shaw, *Revolutionist's Handbook*, 704–5.

20. Plutarch, "Alcibiades," in *Lives*, 4:15 and 4:221.

21. Aristotle, *Politics*, 5.9.6.

22. Adams, October 14, 1771, in *Writings*, 2:251.

23. Stengel, *(You're Too Kind)*, 175–78.

24. Burke, *Reflections on the Revolution in France*, in *Works*, 3:560. Burke, "Thoughts and Details on Scarcity," in *Works*, 5:135.

25. Nietzsche, *Gay Science*, §174; Thoreau, *Walden*, 4.

26. Joinville, *Memoirs*, 60–61.

27. Kant, *Critique of Practical Reason*, 163.

28. Erasmus, *Praise of Folly*, §3; Johnson, *The Rambler*, no. 193, January 21, 1752, 5:246.

6. DANGERS

Epigraph: Johnson, *The Rambler*, no. 114, April 20, 1751, 4:241.

1. Ssu-ma Ch'ien, *Grand Scribe's Records*, 7:291.

2. *Sotah*, 204, citing Rabbi Simeon b-Halafta. The Soncino Talmud translates חלף, *cheleq*, as "flattery," otherwise translated as "hypocrisy" (King James Version) and "impiety" (Jewish Publication Society).

3. Frederick II, *The Anti-Machiavel* (1741), 281. This was translated from

the French edition, *L'anti-Machiavel* (1740), published by Voltaire and for a while attributed to him. Carlyle remarked, "Voltaire's flatteries to Friedrich, in those scattered little Billets with their snatches of verse, are the prettiest in the world, — and approach very near to sincerity, though seldom quite attaining it. Something traceable of false, of suspicious, feline, nearly always, in those seductive warblings; which otherwise are the most melodious bits of idle ingenuity the human brain has ever spun from itself," *History of Friedrich II*, 6:234.

4. As did Ben Jonson in *Volpone, or, The Foxe* (1605). He alludes to the fable of Fox and Crow in act 1, scene 2, and in act 5, scenes 5 and 8.

5. Tacitus, "Pessimum inimicorum genus, laudantes," *Agricola*, §42.

6. Augustine, "On the Words of the Gospel, Matt. X. 16," *Sermones*, no. 64: "Columba amat et quando rixatur: lupus odit et quando blanditur."

7. Tacitus, *Histories*, 2.59; Ammianus Marcellinus, *History*, 27.12.3; Herodian, *History of the Empire*, 2.5; Ammianus Marcellinus, *History*, 29.1.19.

8. Sallust, *War with Jurgutha*, 75.3.

9. Ammianus Marcellinus, *History*, 29.1.11.

10. Fox, *History*, 173.

11. Johnson, "Notes on Macbeth," in *Johnson on Shakespeare*, 8:754.

12. Burke, *A Vindication of Natural Society*, in *Works*, 1:32. Burke refers to Plutarch's "Alexander," §52, in *Lives*, 7:373–75.

13. Plutarch, "How to Tell a Flatterer from a Friend," 267; Stengel, *(You're Too Kind)*, 105.

14. Nietzsche, *Human, All Too Human*, §318; Tacitus, *Annals*, 4.74.

15. Shakespeare, Sonnet 114. Steele, *The Spectator*, December 3, 1711, in Addison and Steele, *Spectator*, 2:258–62; Speer, *Inside the Third Reich*, 83.

16. Cassius Dio, *Roman History*, 67.4.

17. Defoe, *The Dumb Philosopher*, 45; Hazlitt, "On the Disadvantages of Intellectual Superiority," in *Table Talk*, 286–87.

18. Athenaeus, *Deipnosophists*, 6.254b.

19. *Court and Camp of Buonaparte*, 95–96.

20. Stewarton, *Secret Memoirs*, 2:28–29, September 1805.

21. Quoted by Anquetil, *Memoirs*, 1:343.

22. Ribbeck, *Kolax*, 32–33; Glad, "Frank Speech, Flattery, and Friendship," 24–25.

23. Ammianus Marcellinus, *History*, 14.11.11.

24. Cassius Dio, *Roman History*, 37.37.

25. Tacitus, *Histories*, 3.56; Saint-Simon, *Memoirs*, 2:65.

26. Constant, *Recollections*, 2:188; Constant, *Recollections*, 3:165.

27. Motley, *History of the United Netherlands*, 2:324.

28. Retz, *Memoirs*, 123.

29. "Quosdam minus, alios magis veritatem pati," Seneca the Elder, *Suasoriae*, 1.5, speaking of kings.

30. Herodotus, *The Persian Wars*, 7.101. See also Bacon's apothegm on the request of his father, Sir Nicholas Bacon, to Queen Elizabeth I, "Madam, will you have me speak the truth?" *Moral and Historical Works*, 166.

31. Guizot, *History of France*, 4:405.

32. Bordelon, *Management of the Tongue*, 87.

33. Fox, *History*, 47.

34. Shakespeare, *Pericles*, 1.2.38–40; Jonson, *Sejanus*, 1.421.

35. Schiller, *Revolt of the Netherlands*, 109.

36. Tacitus, *Histories*, 2.33; Burke, "An Essay towards an Abridgment of the English History," in *Works*, 7:446–47.

37. Holinshed, *Chronicles*, 1:450.

38. Procopius, *Secret History*, 112, 113.

39. Burke, "Remarks on the Policy of the Allies," in *Works*, 4:432–33.

40. Johnson, *The Idler*, no. 73, September 8, 1759.

41. Bordelon, *Management of the Tongue*, 90.

42. Saint-Simon, *Memoirs*, 2:40–41.

43. Cassius Dio, *Roman History*, 58.18.

44. La Bruyère, *The Characters*, 91–92.

45. Constant, *Recollections*, 1:199.

46. Cicero, *Tusculan Disputations*, 5.21.

47. Gibbon, *Decline and Fall*, 1:959, on Jovian.

48. Holingshed, *Chronicles*, 1:731.

49. See Robinson, "Alexander's Deification," 287n3, 292n20.

50. Parsons, *A Discussion*, 229, 242–45. The ancestor of such events was Moses parting the sea, but as far as we know this had nothing to do with flattery.

51. Kershaw, *Hitler*, 1091.

52. Reimann, *Goebbels*, 3–4.

53. Quoted in Riess, *Joseph Goebbels*, 45; see also Reuth, *Goebbels*, 73.

54. The 2006 edition of the *Guinness Book of World Records* cites Pedro López of Columbia as the "most prolific serial killer"; he murdered more than 300 young girls. The "most prolific murderer" is Behram the Thug of India, who strangled 931 men and women between 1790 and 1840. For its own reasons *Guinness* does not consider Tamerlane or Stalin.

7. HEROISM OF FLATTERY

Epigraph: Erasmus, *Praise of Folly*, §26.

1. Hegel, *Phänomenologie*, 378–79; *Phenomenology*, 310–11.

2. Ribbeck gives a roster of the famous flatterers of ancient Greece in *Kolax*, 76–92.

3. Russell, *Collections and Recollections*, 224.

4. Johnson, *Lives*, 2.40. The poems in question were the *Panegyric* for Cromwell and the *Congratulation* for King Charles.

5. Shelley, "A Defence of Poetry" (written 1821; published 1840).

6. Louis XIV has long been "celebrated for giving pensions to men of genius," but Landor "took the trouble to cast up the amount of several, bestowed on the ornaments of his reign, and found that, collectively, they rather fell short of what Cambacérès was said to give as wages to his cook," Landor, *Charles James Fox*, 170.

7. Saint-Simon, *Memoirs*, 3:217–18.

8. Elizabeth-Charlotte, *Memoirs*, 40. Elizabeth-Charlotte was married for thirty years to Philip d'Orléans, the younger brother of Louis XIV.

9. Montespan, *Secret and Historic Memoirs*, 1:271.

10. La Fontaine, "Au Roi" (1684), in *Oeuvres*, 2:639.

11. Montespan, *Secret and Historic Memoirs*, 2:285.

12. Guizot, *History of France*, 4:396.

13. Guizot, *History of France*, 4:396.

14. La Bruyère, *The Characters*, 299.

15. Talleyrand, *Memoirs*, 1:314.

16. Talleyrand, *Memoirs*, 1:315.

17. Tacitus, *Annals*, 6.18.

18. The Roman ceremony for apotheosis is described in Herodian, *History of the Empire*, 4.3.2 and Cassius Dio, *Roman History*, 74.4.2. The single best study of Roman deification remains Emile Beurlier's *Culte impérial*, which lists seventy-eight persons so honored. For additional numismatic and inscriptional evidence, see Bickermann, "Römische Kaiserapotheose."

19. Arrian, *Anabasis*, 4.10–11.

20. The religious and political complexities of his decision are well examined in C. A. Robinson's "Alexander's Deification."

21. Scott, "Deification of Demetrius Poliorcetes: Part I," 138, and "Part II," 219. On Antony, see Seneca the Elder, *Suasoriae*, 1.6 and Cassius Dio, *Roman History*, 48.31.2.

22. Cicero, *De Natura Deorum*, 2.24.

23. Suetonius, "Julius Caesar," §76, in *Lives of the Caesars*, 1:129; Tacitus, *Annals*, 1.10.

24. Tacitus, *Annals*, 1.77, 3.36.

25. The Roman senate voted officially to name the period between his birth and death the "Augustan Age," Suetonius, "Augustus," §100, in *Lives of the Caesars*, 1:305.

26. Tacitus, *Annals*, 4.37.

27. Cassius Dio, *Roman History*, 59.11.

28. Suetonius, "Claudius," §11 and §45, in *Lives of the Caesars*, 2:21 and 2:79.

29. Tacitus, *Annals*, 15.23; Cassius Dio, *Roman History*, 63.26.

30. Suetonius, "Domitian," §13, in *Lives of the Caesars*, 2:348; Aurelius Victor, *De Caesaribus*, 13.

31. Cassius Dio, *Roman History*, 70.1; *Scriptores Historiae Augustae*, 1:19, 43, 45, and 81.

32. *Scriptores Historiae Augustae*, 2:161.

33. Suetonius, "Caligula," §22, in *Lives of the Caesars*, 1:449.

34. Suetonius, "Vitellius," §2, in *Lives of the Caesars*, 2:239–41. According to Tacitus, Vitellius "is regarded today as a type of obsequious ignominy," *Annals*, 6.32.

35. *Scriptores Historiae Augustae*, 2:37.

36. Cassius Dio, *Roman History*, 78.9.2; *Scriptores Historiae Augustae*, 2:29 and 59.

37. Appian, *The Civil Wars*, 2:148.

38. Josephus, *Jewish Antiquities*, 19. 343–50.

39. "Justin Martyr, "Apology 1," §21; Tertullian, "Apology," §34.

40. Beurlier, *Culte impérial*, 271–72.

41. In the Vulgate, Psalm 81:6: "Ego dixi dii estis et filii Excelsi omnes." Nispel's article "Christian Deification" examines early Christian interpretation of the verse.

42. Clement of Alexandria, *Exhortation to the Heathen*, 1.8.4; Gregory Nazianzen, "The Third Theological Oration" [Oration 29], in *Select Orations*, 308. On *theosis*, or "deification," see Pelikan, *Emergence of the Catholic Tradition*, 155. For the spread and development of *theosis*, see Russell, *The Doctrine of Deification*.

43. Procopius, *Secret History*, 107. Justinian would recognize the flattering allusion to Romulus, who was thought to have ascended to the gods while performing a rite; see Plutarch, "Romulus," §27, in *Lives*, 1:177.

8. TO FLATTER GOD

Epigraph: White, *History of the Warfare of Science with Theology*, 372.

1. Franklin, *Writings*, 83. For more on Franklin's religion, see Walters, *Benjamin Franklin and His Gods*.

2. Franklin, *Writings*, 84–85.

3. *Rig Veda*, 8.19.1; *Bhagavad Gītā*, 11.36; *Mahābhārata*, 6.33.36.

4. The Jewish tradition emphasizes that all things, not just people, praise God. See Ginzberg, *Legends of the Jews*, 5:61–62.

5. Plato, *Laws*, 12.948c, in *Collected Dialogues*, 1494.

6. Varty, *Reynard, Renart, Reinaert*, 68–84.

7. "Tvatsambhāvitam ātmānam / bahu manyāmahe vayam," Kālidāsa, *The Birth of Kumara*, 214–15.

8. Kant, *Religion within the Limits of Reason Alone*, 186.

9. Version B of the Anglo-Saxon *Genesis*, in Gordon, *Anglo-Saxon Poetry*, 100–101.

10. Halifax, *Complete Works*, 251.

11. Tertullian, "On Modesty," 76.

12. For a study of the human heart in Christian icons and theology, see Doueihi, *Histoire perverse*.

13. Words and music by Cleland B. McAfee, 1901; McAfee was a Presbyterian minister who taught theology at McCormick Seminary in Chicago. *Heart of God* is also the title of a poem by Vachel Lindsay and of a book by Nobel Laureate Rabindranath Tagore.

14. Theophilus, *Theophilus to Autolycus*, 103.

15. Marcus Aurelius, *Meditations*, 10.8.

16. For examination of the historical sources, see Gero, *Byzantine Iconoclasm during the Reign of Leo III* and *Byzantine Iconoclasm during the Reign of Constantine V*, and Krumbacher, *Geschichte der byzantinischen Litteratur*.

17. See Schönborn, *L'icône du Christ*, 30–53.

18. Gibbon, *Decline and Fall*, 3:95–96.

19. Gibbon, *Decline and Fall*, 3:93.

20. Figurines of a skiing and running Jesus are currently marketed by Catholic Supply of St. Louis. In *Undefeated* Kentucky painter Steven S. Sawyer depicted Jesus as a buffed-up boxer.

21. Cicero, *De Natura Deorum*, 1.27. In "An Apology for Raymond Sebond," Montaigne quotes Cicero and comments, "That is why Xenophanes said with a smile that if the beasts invent god for themselves, as they prob-

ably do, they certainly make them like themselves," *Essays*, 597. See also William Butler Yeats's "The Indian upon God."

22. Cicero, *De Natura Deorum*, 2.17.

23. Late in life, Franklin admitted "Doubts as to his Divinity" in a letter to Ezra Stiles (March 9, 1790), in *Writings*, 1179.

24. Feuerbach, *Essence of Christianity*, xxxvii–xxxviii.

25. Feuerbach, *Essence of Christianity*, 51; the quotation is taken from Augustine's Sermon 371, "De Nativitate Domini, III," which in turn is taken from Athanasius, *De Incarnatione Verbi Dei*, §54.

26. Feuerbach, *Essence of Christianity*, 249.

27. Feuerbach, *Essence of Christianity*, 47.

28. Feuerbach, *Essence of Christianity*, 35–36.

29. Feuerbach, *Essence of Christianity*, 53.

30. Feuerbach, *Essence of Christianity*, 121–23.

31. Feuerbach, *Essence of Christianity*, 136.

32. Philostratus, *Life of Apollonius of Tyana*, 1.11; see also 4.40.

33. In the Gospel of Luke, 11:1–4, Jesus gives his disciples the model but not the preliminary instructions.

34. Christian theologians observed that Jesus's instruction did not require that *all* prayer be private. For discussions on the interiority of prayer, see Benson and Wirzba, *Phenomenology of Prayer*.

35. Nock, "Deification and Julian," 115.

36. *Scriptores Historiae Augustae*, 1:193.

37. Cassius Dio, *Roman History*, 72.9.

38. *Yoma*, 69b. Ismar Schorsch, "Parashah Commentary," October 19, 2002, Jewish Theological Seminary, http://learn.jtsa.edu/topics/parashah/5763/lekhlekha.shtml.

9. FAREWELL

Epigraph: Tolstoy, *War and Peace*, 23.

BIBLIOGRAPHY

Bracketed dates indicate first publication date, when known.

Adams, Henry. *History of the United States of America during the Administrations of Thomas Jefferson*. New York: Library of America, 1986 [1889–90].

Adams, Samuel. *The Writings of Samuel Adams*. Edited by Harry Alonzo Cushing. 4 vols. New York: G. P. Putnam's Sons, 1906.

Addison, Joseph, and Richard Steele. *The Spectator*. Edited by G. Gregory Smith. 4 vols. London: J. M. Dent, 1907 [1711–12].

Aesop. *Aesop's Fables*. Translated by Laura Gibbs. Oxford: Oxford University Press, 2002. See also Croxall and l'Estrange.

Alciati, Andrea. *Emblemata*. Lugduni [Lyons]: Gulielmi Rouillii, 1600 [1522].

Ammianus Marcellinus. *The History*. Translated by John Rolfe, 3 vols. Cambridge: Harvard University Press, 1935–39 [c. AD 391].

Aneau, Barthélemy. *Imagination poétique, traduicte en vers François, des Latins, & Grecz, par l'auteur mesme d'iceux*. Lyons: Par Macé Bonhomme, 1552.

Anquetil, Louis-Pierre. *Memoirs of the Court of France during the Reign of Louis XIV*. 2 vols. Edinburgh: Bell & Bradfute, 1791.

Appian. *The Civil Wars*. Translated by Horace A. White. 2 vols. Cambridge: Harvard University Press, 1913 [c. AD 150].

Aristophanes. *The Eleven Comedies*. 2 vols. New York: Horace Liveright, 1943 [424–388 BC].

Aristotle. *Nicomachean Ethics*. Translated by H. Rackham. Cambridge: Harvard University Press, 1936 [c. 330 BC].

———. *Politics*. Translated by H. Rackham. Cambridge: Harvard University Press, 1936 [c. 335 BC].

Arrian. *Anabasis*. Translated by P. A. Brunt. 2 vols. Cambridge: Harvard University Press, 1976 [c. AD 150].

Ash, John. *New and Complete Dictionary of the English Language*. 2nd ed. 2 vols. London: Vernor & Hood, 1795.

Athenaeus. *The Deipnosophists*. Translated by Charles Burton Gulick. 7 vols. Cambridge: Harvard University Press, 1927–57 [c. AD 228].

Augustine. *Sermones ad populum.* Vol. 38 of *Patrologia Latina*, editio novissima. Paris: J.-P. Migne, 1865.

Aurelius Victor, Sextus. *De Caesaribus.* Translated by H. W. Bird. Liverpool: Liverpool University Press, 1994 [c. AD 360].

Babrius and Phaedrus. Edited and translated by Ben Edwin Perry. Cambridge: Harvard University Press, 1965.

Bacon, Francis. *The Moral and Historical Works of Lord Bacon.* Edited by Joseph Devey. London: George Bell & Sons, 1884.

Balzac, Honoré de. *Eugénie Grandet.* Translated by Ellen Marriage. Philadelphia: Gebbie, 1899 [1833].

———. *The Physiology of Marriage.* Translator unknown. Baltimore: Johns Hopkins University Press, 1997 [1829].

———. "The Reproach." In *Droll Stories,* 173–83. Translator unknown. New York: Modern Library, 1930 [1837].

Beethoven, Ludwig van. *Ludwig van Beethovens Konversationshefte.* Edited by Karl-Heinz Koehler and Grita Herre. 11 vols. Leipzig: VEB Deutscher Verlag für Musik, 1968–.

Benson, Bruce Ellis, and Norma Wirzba, eds. *The Phenomenology of Prayer.* New York: Fordham University Press, 2005.

Besançon, Alain. *The Forbidden Image: An Intellectual History of Iconoclasm.* Translated by Jane Marie Todd. Chicago: University of Chicago Press, 2000 [1994].

Beurlier, Emile. *Le culte impérial: Son histoire et son organization depuis Auguste jusqu'a Justinien.* Paris: Ernest Thorin, 1891.

Bickermann, Elias. "Die Römische Kaiserapotheose." *Archive für Religionswissenschaft* 27 (1929): 1–34.

Bismarck, Otto von. *Bismarck: The Man and the Statesman, Being the Reflections and Reminiscences of Otto Prince von Bismarck.* Translated by A. J. Butler. 2 vols. London: Smith, Elder, 1898.

Blackwell, Thomas. *Memoirs of the Court of Augustus.* 2 vols. Edinburgh: Hamilton, Balfour, & Neill, 1753.

Bordelon, Laurent. *The Management of the Tongue.* London: D. Leach, for H. Rhodes, 1706.

Bourrienne, Louis Antoine Fauvelet de. *Memoirs of Napoleon Bonaparte.* Edited by R. W. Phipps. 4 vols. New York: Charles Scribner's Sons, 1891 [1829–31].

Bowen, Marjorie. "The Art of Flattery." In *World's Wonder and Other Essays,* 117–38. London: Hutchinson, 1938.

Burke, Edmund. *Works*. 12 vols. London: Nimmo, 1899.

Burr, Aaron. *Memoirs*. Edited by Matthew L. Davis. 2 vols. New York: Da Capo, 1971 [1836].

Carlyle, Thomas. *History of Friedrich II of Prussia, Called Frederick the Great*. 10 vols. London: Chapman & Hall, 1873 [1858–65].

Cassius Dio Cocceianus. *Dio's Roman History*. Translated by Earnest Cary, on the basis of the version of Herbert Baldwin Foster. 9 vols. Cambridge: Harvard University Press, 1914–27 [AD 200–222].

Catherine the Great. *Memoirs*. Translated by Moura Budberg. London: Hamish Hamilton, 1955 [1859].

Cervantes, Miguel de. *The Adventures of Don Quixote*. Translated by J. M. Cohen. New York: Barnes & Noble, 1999 [1604].

Chambry, Aemilius. *Aesopi Fabulae*. 2 vols. Paris: Société d'édition "Les Belles Lettres," 1925–26.

Chesterfield, Philip Dormer Stanhope, 4th Earl of. *Letters to His Son*. 2 vols. Washington DC: M. Walter Dunne, 1901 [1774].

Cicero, Marcus Tullius. "De Amicitia." Translated by William Armistead Falconer. In *Cicero*, 20:101–211. Cambridge: Harvard University Press, 1927 [44 BC].

———. *De Natura Deorum*. Translated by H. Rackham. Cambridge: Harvard University Press, 1933 [45 BC].

———. *Tusculan Disputations*. 2nd ed. Translated by J. E. King. Cambridge: Harvard University Press, 1945 [45 BC].

Clement of Alexandria. *Exhortation to the Heathen*. Translated by W. Wilson. In *The Ante-Nicene Fathers*, edited by A. Cleveland Coxe, 2:171–206. New York: Christian Literature, 1885 [c. AD 200].

Colton, Charles Caleb. *Lacon; or, Many Things in Few Words Addressed to Those Who Think*. Rev. ed. New York: Charles Wells, 1836 [1820].

Commentariolum Petitionis. Sometimes attributed to Quintus Cicero, brother of the orator. Translated by Mary Isobel Henderson as *Handbook of Electioneering*, in *Letters to His Brother*, 750–91. Cambridge: Harvard University Press, 1972 [c. 60 BC].

Confucius. *Confucian Analects*. Translated by James Legge. Oxford: Oxford University Press, 1893 [c. 480 BC].

Constant [Louis Constant Wairy]. *Recollections of the Private Life of Napoleon Bonaparte*. 3 vols. Akron: Saalfield, 1902 [1830].

Court and Camp of Buonaparte. London: John Murray, 1829.

Crabbe, George. "The Birth of Flattery." In *Poems*, 3rd ed., 191–207. London: J. Hatchard, 1808.

Croxall, Samuel. *Fables of Aesop, with Instructive Applications*. Halifax: William Milner, 1848 [1722].

Defoe, Daniel. *The Dumb Philosopher; or, Great Britain's Wonder: Containing a Faithful and Very Surprising Account How Dickory Cronke, a Tinner's Son in the County of Cornwall, was born Dumb and Continued so for Fifty-Eight Years; and How some Days before he died, he came to his Speech; with Memoirs of His Life. And the Manner of his Death*. London: Thomas Bickerton, 1719.

Diogenes Laertius. *Lives of Eminent Philosophers*. Translated by R. D. Hicks. 2 vols. Cambridge: Harvard University Press, 1925 [c. AD 250].

Doris, Charles. *Secret Memoirs of Napoleon Buonaparte*. 2 vols. London: H. Colburn and Longman, Hurst, Rees, & Orme, 1815.

Doueihi, Milad. *Histoire perverse du coeur humain*. Paris: Seuil, 1996. Translated by the author as *A Perverse History of the Human Heart*. Cambridge: Harvard University Press, 1998.

Dryden, John. *The Works of Virgil*. Oxford: Oxford University Press, 1961 [1697].

Elizabeth-Charlotte [Wittelsbach von Pfalz], Duchesse d'Orléans. *Memoirs of the Court of Louis XIV and of the Regency*. Boston: L. C. Page, 1899 [1889].

Emerson, Ralph Waldo. *The Conduct of Life*. In *Essays and Lectures*, 937–1124. New York: Library of America, 1983 [1860].

———. "Gifts." In *Essays: Second Series*. In *Essays and Lectures*, 533–38. New York: Library of America, 1983 [1844].

———. *Representative Men*. In *Essays and Lectures*, 611–761. New York: Library of America, 1983 [1850].

Engberg-Pedersen, Troels. "Plutarch to Prince Philopappus on How to Tell a Flatterer from a Friend." In *Friendship, Flattery, and Frankness of Speech: Studies on Friendship in the New Testament World*, edited by John T. Fitzgerald, 61–79. Leiden: E. J. Brill, 1996.

Erasmus, Desiderius. *Praise of Folly*. Translated by Betty Radice. Harmondsworth: Penguin, 1971 [1511].

Fay, Laurel E. *Shostakovich: A Life*. New York: Oxford University Press, 2000.

Feuerbach, Ludwig. *The Essence of Christianity*. Translated by George Eliot. New York: Harper & Row, 1957 [1841].

Fitzgerald, John T., ed. *Friendship, Flattery, and Frankness of Speech: Studies on Friendship in the New Testament World*. Leiden: E. J. Brill, 1996.

Flaubert, Gustave. *The Dictionary of Accepted Ideas.* Translated by Jacques Barzun. New York: New Directions, 1968 [1951; the *Dictionnaire* was left unfinished when Flaubert died in 1880].

Fox, Charles James. *History of the Early Part of the Reign of James the Second.* London: William Miller, 1808.

Franklin, Benjamin. *Writings.* Edited by J. A. Leo Lemay. New York: Library of America, 1987.

Frederick II, King of Prussia. *Anti-Machiavel; or, An Examination of Machiavel's Prince.* London: T. Woodward, 1741 [1740].

Fulwell, Ulpian. *Ars Adulandi, the Art of Flattery: A Critical Edition.* Edited by Roberta Buchanan. Salzburg: Institut für Anglistik und Amerikanistik, Universität Salzburg, 1984 [1576].

Geoffrey of Monmouth. *The History of the Kings of Britain.* Translated by Lewis Thorpe. Harmondsworth: Penguin, 1966 [1136].

Gero, Stephen. *Byzantine Iconoclasm during the Reign of Constantine V.* Louvain: Corpus Scriptorum Christianorum Orientalium, 1977.

———. *Byzantine Iconoclasm during the Reign of Leo III.* Louvain: Corpus Scriptorum Christianorum Orientalium, 1973.

Gibbon, Edward. *The Autobiography.* Edited by Dero A. Saunders. New York: Meridian, 1961 [1796].

———. *The Decline and Fall of the Roman Empire.* Edited by David Womersley. 3 vols. New York: Viking Penguin, 1995 [1776, 1781, 1788].

Ginzberg, Louis. *The Legends of the Jews.* 7 vols. Baltimore: Johns Hopkins University Press, 1998 [1909–38].

Glad, Clarence E. "Frank Speech, Flattery, and Friendship in Philodemus." In *Friendship, Flattery, and Frankness of Speech: Studies on Friendship in the New Testament World,* edited by John T. Fitzgerald, 21–59. Leiden: E. J. Brill, 1996.

Gleason, Judith. *Leaf and Bone: African Praise-Poems.* New York: Viking, 1980.

Goethe, Johann Wolfgang von. *The Autobiography.* Translated by John Oxenford. New York: Horizon, 1969 [1833].

———. *Reineke Fuchs,* with illustrations by Wilhelm von Kaulbach. Stuttgart: J. G. Cotta'scher Verlag, 1846 [1794]. Translated by David Vedder as *The Story of Reynard the Fox,* with illustrations by Gustav Jacob Canton. London: W. S. Orr, 1852.

Gordon, R. K. *Anglo-Saxon Poetry.* London: J. M. Dent, 1926.

Government of the Tongue. Oxford: At the Theater, 1667.

Gregory Nazianzen. *Select Orations*. Translated by Charles Gordon Browne and James Edward Swallow. In *Nicene and Post-Nicene Fathers*, edited by Philip Schaff and Henry Wace, 7:203–434. Buffalo: Christian Literature, 1894 [c. AD 380].

Guizot, François, and Madame Guizot De Witt. *The History of France, from the Earliest Times to 1848*. Translated by Robert Black. 8 vols. New York: J. B Alden, 1885 [1870–75].

Halifax, George. *The Complete Works of George Savile, First Marquess of Halifax*. Oxford: Clarendon, 1912.

Hamilton, Alexander. *Writings*. Edited by Roger Hertog and Susan Hertog. New York: Library of America, 2001.

Hamori, Andras. *The Art of Flattery: Form and Argument in a Panegyric by al-Mutanabbi*. Tel Aviv: Tel Aviv University, 1985.

Harflete, Henry. *The Hunting of the Fox; or, Flattery Displayed*. London: A. Mathewes, for Philemon Stephens and Christopher Meredith, 1632.

Hazlitt, William. *Table Talk*. London: J. B. Dent & Sons, 1908 [1821–22].

Hegel, George W. F. *Lectures on the Philosophy of Religion*. Edited by Peter C. Hodgson. Translated by R. F. Brown, P. C. Hodgson, and J. M. Stewart. 3 vols. Berkeley: University of California Press, 1984–87.

———. *Phänomenologie des Geistes*. Frankfurt: Suhrkamp, 1986 [1807]. Translated by A. V. Miller as *Hegel's Phenomenology of Spirit*. Oxford: Oxford University Press, 1977.

Herodian. *History of the Empire from the Time of Marcus Aurelius*. Translated by C. R. Whittaker. 2 vols. Cambridge: Harvard University Press, 1970 [c. AD 240].

Herodotus. *The Persian Wars*. Translated by A. D. Godley. 4 vols. Cambridge: Harvard University Press, 1920–25 [c. 430 BC].

Hertel, Johannes. *The Panchatantra: A Collection of Ancient Hindu Tales in the Recension, Called Panchakhyanaka, and Dated 1199 A.D., of the Jaina Monk, Purnabhadra*. Harvard Oriental Series, vol. 11. Cambridge: Harvard University Press, 1908. Translated by Arthur W. Ryder as *The Panchatantra*. Chicago: University of Chicago Press, 1925.

Hobbes, Thomas. *Leviathan*. Edited by Michael Oakeshott. New York: Collier, 1962 [1651].

Holinshed, Raphael. *Holinshed's Chronicles of England, Scotland, and Ireland*. Edited by Sir Henry Ellis. 6 vols. London: J. Johnson; F. C. & J. Rivington; T. Payne, Wilkie & Robinson; Longman, Hurst, Rees, & Orme; Cadell & Davies; and J. Mawman, 1807–8 [1577–86].

Holmes, Oliver Wendell. *The Professor at the Breakfast Table*. Boston: Houghton Mifflin, 1883 [1860].

Howarth, Herbert. "Puzzle of Flattery." In *The Tiger's Heart: Eight Essays on Shakespeare*, 120–42. New York: Oxford University Press, 1970.

Hume, David. *A Treatise of Human Nature*. Oxford: Oxford University Press, 1965 [1739].

Huxley, Aldous. *Grey Eminence*. New York: Harper & Row, 1966 [1941].

———. *Point Counter Point*. New York: Harper & Row, 1965 [1928].

Isaacson, Walter. *Kissinger: A Biography*. New York: Simon & Schuster, 1992.

Jacobs, Joseph. *History of the Aesopic Fable*. Vol. 1 of *The Fables of Aesop as first printed by William Caxton in 1484*. London: D. Nutt, 1889.

Jefferson, Thomas. "A Summary View of the Rights of British America." In *Writings*, edited by Merrill D. Peterson, 103–22. New York: Library of America, 1984 [1774].

Johnson, Samuel. *A Dictionary of the English Language*. 2 vols. London: J. Knapton et al., 1756.

———. *The Idler and The Adventurer*. Vol. 2 of *The Yale Edition of the Works of Samuel Johnson*. Edited by W. J. Bate, John M. Bullitt, and L. F. Powell. New Haven: Yale University Press, 1963 [1758–60 and 1753–54].

———. *Johnson on Shakespeare*. Vols. 7 and 8 of *The Yale Edition of the Works of Samuel Johnson*. Edited by Arthur Sherbo. New Haven: Yale University Press, 1968.

———. *Lives of the English Poets*. Edited by Roger Lonsdale. 4 vols. Oxford: Oxford University Press, 2006 [1779–81].

———. *The Rambler*. Vols. 3, 4, and 5 of *The Yale Edition of the Works of Samuel Johnson*. Edited by W. J. Bate and Albrecht B. Strauss. New Haven: Yale University Press, 1969 [1750–52].

Joinville, François Ferdinand Philippe d'Orléans, Prince de. *Memoirs*. Translated by Lady Mary Loyd. New York: Macmillan, 1895 [1894].

Jonson, Ben. *Poems*. Edited by George Burke Johnston. Cambridge: Harvard University Press, 1968.

———. *Sejanus*. Edited by Jonas A. Barish. New Haven: Yale University Press, 1965 [1603].

———. *Timber; or, Discoveries*. London: J. M. Dent & Sons, 1951 [1641].

———. *Volpone*. Edited by Philip Brockbank. New York: Hill & Wang, 1968 [1605].

Josephus. *The Jewish Antiquities*. Translated by H. St. J. Thackeray and Louis

H. Feldman. 8 vols. Cambridge: Harvard University Press, 1930–65 [c. AD 100].

Justin Martyr. "Apology I." Translated by Philip Schaff. In *The Ante-Nicene Fathers,* vol. 1, *The Apostolic Fathers—Justin Martyr—Irenaeus,* edited by Alexander Roberts and James Donaldson, 163–87. New York: Christian Literature, 1890 [c. AD 155].

Juvenal. *Satires.* Translated by G. G. Ramsay. In *Juvenal and Persius,* 1–307. Cambridge: Harvard University Press, 1918 [c. AD 100].

Kālidāsa. *The Birth of Kumāra.* Translated by David Smith. New York: New York University Press, 2005 [c. 5th century AD].

Kammen, Michael. *Mystic Chords of Memory: The Transformation of Tradition in American Culture.* New York: Knopf, 1991.

Kant, Immanuel. *Critique of Practical Reason.* Translated by Lewis White Beck. Indianapolis: Bobbs-Merrill, 1956 [1788].

———. *Religion within the Limits of Reason Alone.* Translated by Theodore M. Greene and Hoyt H. Hudson. New York: Harper & Row, 1960 [1793].

Kautilya. *The Arthashastra.* Translated by L. N. Rangarajan. New Delhi: Penguin, 1992 [c. AD 150].

Keim, Albert, and Louis Lumet. *Honoré de Balzac.* Translated by Frederic Taber Cooper. New York: Fredrick A. Stokes, 1914.

Kershaw, Ian. *Hitler, 1936–1945: Nemesis.* New York: W. W. Norton, 2000.

Kokott, Hartmut. *Reynke de Vos.* Munich: Wilhelm Fink Verlag, 1981.

Kooser, Ted. *The Poetry Home Repair Manual.* Lincoln: University of Nebraska Press, 2005.

Krumbacher, Karl. *Geschichte der byzantischen Litteratur von Justinian bis zum Ende des oströmischen Reiches, 527–1453.* 2nd ed. Munich: Beck, 1897 [1891].

La Bruyère, Jean de. *The Characters; or, The Manners of the Age.* Translated by Henri van Laun. London: George Routledge & Sons, 1929 [1688].

La Fayette, Marie-Madeleine Pioche de la Vergne, Comtesse de. *Memoirs of the Court of France for the Years 1688–1689.* Translated by J. M. Shelmerdine. London: George Routledge & Sons, 1929 [1731].

La Fontaine, Jean de. *Oeuvres complètes.* Edited by Pierre Clarac. 2 vols. Paris: Gallimard, 1958. The fables are translated by Norman Shapiro as *The Complete Fables of La Fontaine.* Urbana: University of Illinois Press, 2007.

Lamb, Charles. *The Complete Works and Letters.* New York: Modern Library, 1935.

———. *Prince Dorus; or, Flattery Put Out of Countenance*. London: M. J. Godwin, 1811.

Landor, Walter Savage. *Charles James Fox*. Edited by Stephen Wheeler. London: John Murray, 1907 [1812].

La Rochefoucauld, François VI de. *Maximes*. Edited by Jacques Truchet. Paris: Éditions Garnier Frères, 1967 [1664]. Translated by Louis Kronenberger as *Maxims*. New York: Random House, 1959.

Le Roy Ladurie, Emmanuel. *Saint-Simon and the Court of Louis XIV*. Translated by Arthur Goldhammer. Chicago: University of Chicago Press, 2001 [1997].

Le Sage, Alain René. *The Adventures of Gil Blas of Santillane*. Translated by Tobias Smollett. Philadelphia: J. B. Lippincott, 1876 [1715–35; Smollett translation, 1749].

L'Estrange, Roger. *Fables, of Aesop and other Eminent Mythologists: With Morals and Reflexions*. London: R. Sare, T. Sawbridge, B. Took, M. Gillyflower, A. & J. Churchil, & J. Hindmarsh, 1692.

Lichtheim, Miriam. *Ancient Egyptian Literature*. 3 vols. Berkeley: University of California Press, 1973, 1976, and 1980.

Loyseau, Charles. *A Treatise of Orders and Plain Dignities*. Edited and translated by Howell A. Lloyd. Cambridge: Cambridge University Press, 1994 [1610].

Lucian. *The Works of Lucian of Samosata*. Translated by H. W. Fowler and F. G. Fowler. 4 vols. Oxford: Clarendon, 1905 [2nd century AD].

Macaulay, Thomas Babington. *Critical and Historical Essays*. 2 vols. London: J. M. Dent, 1907.

———. *The History of England from the Accession of James II*. 5 vols. New York: Wm. L. Allison, n.d. [1848].

Machiavelli. *The Prince*. Translated by Peter Bondanella and Mark Musa. In *The Portable Machiavelli*, 77–166. New York: Penguin, 1979 [1513].

Macklin, Charles. *The Man of the World*. Los Angeles: Augustan Reprint Society, 1951 [1792].

Madison, James. *Writings*. Edited by Jack N. Rackove. New York: Library of America, 1999.

Mandeville, Bernard. *The Fable of the Bees; or, Private Vices, Publick Benefits*. 2 vols. Oxford: Clarendon, 1924 [1714, 1729].

Marcovich, Miroslav. "How to Flatter Women: P. Oxy. 2891." *Classical Philology* 70 (April 1975): 123–24.

Marcus Aurelius. *Meditations*. In *Marcus Aurelius*, edited and translated by C. R. Haines, 1–343. Rev. ed. Harvard University Press, 1930 [c. AD 174].

Marguerite de Valois. *Mémoires*. Edited by Paul Bonnefon. Paris: Éditions Bossard, 1920 [1628].

Marie de France. *Fables*. Edited and translated by Harriet Spiegel. Toronto: University of Toronto Press, 1987 [between 1160 and 1190].

Marin, Louis. *Portrait of the King*. Translated by Martha M. Houle. Minneapolis: University of Minnesota Press, 1988 [1981].

Masson, Charles François Philibert. *Secret Memoirs of the Court of Petersburg*. 2 vols. London: Longman & Rees, 1800.

Méneval, Baron Claude-François de. *Memoirs of Napoleon Bonaparte: The Court of the First Empire*. 3 vols. New York: P. F. Collier & Son, 1910 [1894].

Meredith, George. *The Egoist*. Edited by Robert M. Adams. New York: W. W. Norton, 1979 [1879].

Milton, John. *Areopagitica*. In *Complete Prose Works of John Milton*, edited by Ernest Sirluck, 2:480–570. New Haven: Yale University Press, 1959 [1644].

Montaigne, Michel de. *The Essays of Michel de Montaigne*. Translated by M. A. Screech. London: Penguin, 1991 [1580, 1582, 1588].

Montespan, Madame la Marquise de. *Secret and Historic Memoirs of the Courts of France*. 2 vols. Philadelphia: Rittenhouse, 1904.

The Most Delectable History of Reynard the Fox. London: Elizabeth All-de, 1629.

Motley, John Lothrop. *History of the United Netherlands*. 4 vols. London: John Murray, 1868.

Nietzsche, Friedrich. *The Gay Science*. Translated by Walter Kaufman. New York: Random House, 1974 [1882].

———. *Human, All Too Human*. Translated by Marion Faber. Lincoln: University of Nebraska Press, 1984 [1878].

———. *The Portable Nietzsche*. Translated by Walter Kaufman. New York: Viking, 1954.

Nispel, Mark D. "Christian Deification and the Early Testimonia." *Virgiliae Christianae* 53 (August 1999): 289–304.

Nock, Arthur Darby. "Deification and Julian: I." *Journal of Roman Studies* 47, nos. 1–2 (1957): 115–23.

Parsons, Robert, S.J. *A Discussion of the Answere of M. William Barlow, D. of Divinity, to the Booke intituled: The Judgement of a Catholike Englishman living in banishment for his Religion &c*. Saint-Omer: English College Press, 1612.

Pascal, Blaise. *Pensées: Thoughts on Religion and Other Subjects.* Translated by William Finlayson Trotter. New York: Washington Square, 1965 [1670].

Pelikan, Jaroslav. *The Emergence of the Catholic Tradition (100–600).* Chicago: University of Chicago Press, 1971.

Perry, Ben E. *Aesopica.* Urbana: University of Illinois Press, 1952.

Phaedrus. See Babrius.

Philostratus. *The Life of Apollonius of Tyana.* Translated by F. C. Conybeare. 2 vols. Cambridge: Harvard University Press, 1912 [c. AD 217].

Plato. *The Collected Dialogues.* Edited by Edith Hamilton and Huntington Cairns. Princeton: Princeton University Press, 1961 [early 4th century BC].

The Pleasant History of Reynard the Fox. Translated by Thomas Roscoe. Illustrated by A. T. Elwes and John Jellicoe. London: Sampson Low, Marston, Low, & Searle, 1873.

Pliny, the Younger. *Letters and Panegyricus.* Translated by Betty Radice. 2 vols. Cambridge: Harvard University Press, 1969 [c. AD 99–110].

Plochmann, George Kimball, and Franklin E. Robinson. *A Friendly Companion to Plato's Gorgias.* Carbondale: Southern Illinois University Press, 1988.

Plutarch. "How to Tell a Flatterer from a Friend." In *Moralia,* translated by Frank Cole Babbitt, 1:261–395. Cambridge: Harvard University Press, 1927 [c. AD 110–120].

———. *Lives.* Translated by Bernadotte Perrin. 11 vols. Cambridge: Harvard University Press, 1914–26 [c. AD 100–120].

Pope, Alexander. "An Epistle to Dr. Arbuthnot." In *The Poems of Alexander Pope,* edited by John Butt, 597–612. New Haven: Yale University Press, 1963 [1735].

Procopius. *The Secret History.* Translated by G. A. Williamson. Harmondsworth: Penguin, 1966 [c. AD 550].

Publilius Syrus. *Sententiae.* In *Minor Latin Poets,* edited by J. Wight Duff and Arnold M. Duff, 1–111. Cambridge: Harvard University Press, 1954 [1st century BC].

Raleigh, Sir Walter, Lord Treasurer Burleigh, Cardinal Sermonetta, and Mr. [Edward] Walsingham. *Instructions for Youth, Gentlemen and Noblemen.* London: Randal Minshull, 1722.

Reimann, Viktor. *Goebbels.* Translated by Stephen Wendt. Garden City NY: Doubleday, 1976 [1971].

Retz, Cardinal de [John Francis Paul de Gondi]. *Memoirs.* Boston: Grolier Society, 1905 [1717].

Reuth, Ralf Georg. *Goebbels.* Translated by Krishna Winston. New York: Harcourt Brace, 1993 [1990].

Ribbeck, O. *Kolax: Eine ethologische Studie.* Leipzig: S. Hirzel, 1883.

Riess, Curt. *Joseph Goebbels.* London: Hollis & Carter, 1949.

Robinson, C. A., Jr. "Alexander's Deification." *American Journal of Philology* 63, no. 3 (1943): 286–301.

Rousseau, Jean-Jacques. *Emile.* Translated by Barbara Foxley. London: J. M. Dent & Sons, 1972 [1762].

Russell, George William Erskine. *Collections and Recollections.* New York and London: Harper & Brothers, 1898. Published under the pseudonym "One Who Has Kept a Diary."

Russell, Norman. *The Doctrine of Deification in the Greek Patristic Tradition.* Cambridge: Cambridge University Press, 2004.

Saint-Simon. *Memoirs of Louis XIV.* Translated by Bayle St. John. 4 vols. New York: James Pott, 1901 [1739–50].

Sallust. *War with Jurgutha.* In *Sallust,* translated by J. C. Rolfe, 131–381. Cambridge: Harvard University Press, 1921 [c. 35 BC].

Schiller, Friedrich. *The Revolt of the United Netherlands.* Translated by A. J. W. Morrison and L. Dora Schmitz. London: George Bell & Sons, 1897 [1788].

Schlegel, Augustus. *Course of Lectures on Dramatic Art and Literature.* Translated by John Black, revised by A. J. W. Morrison. London: Henry G. Bohn, 1846 [1808].

Schönborn, Christoph. *L'icône du Christ: Fondements théologiques.* Paris: Éditions du Cerf, 1986.

Scott, Kenneth. "The Deification of Demetrius Poliorcetes: Part I." *American Journal of Philology* 49, no. 2 (1928): 137–66.

———. "The Deification of Demetrius Poliorcetes: Part II." *American Journal of Philology* 49, no. 3 (1928): 217–39.

Scott, Sir Walter. "The Lay of the Last Minstrel." In *Poetical Works,* edited by J. Logie Robertson, 1–88. Oxford: Oxford University Press, 1904 [1805].

Scriptores Historiae Augustae. Translated by David Magie. 3 vols. Cambridge: Harvard University Press, 1921–32.

Seneca, Lucius Annaues. *Suasoriae.* Translated by Michael Winterbottom. In *The Elder Seneca,* 2:484–611. Cambridge: Harvard University Press, 1992 [c. 40 BC].

Shaw, George Bernard. *The Revolutionist's Handbook and Pocket Companion.* In *Complete Plays with Prefaces,* 3:687–743. New York: Dodd, Mead, 1963 [1905].

Shelley, Percy Bysshe. "On the Punishment of Death." In *Essays and Letters*, 64–71. London: Walter Scott, 1887.

Shestov, Leo. *All Things Are Possible*. Translated by S. S. Kotaliansky. London: Martin Secker, 1920 [1905].

Sidney, Sir Philip. *Astrophil and Stella*. Edited by Max Putzel. New York: Anchor, 1967 [1598].

Simrock, Karl. *Gedichte*. Leipzig: Hahn'schen Verlag, 1844.

Smith, Andrew. *The Turkey*. Champaign: University of Illinois Press, 2006.

Soṭah. Translated by A. Cohen. London: Soncino, 1936.

Speer, Albert. *Inside the Third Reich*. Translated by Richard Winston and Clara Winston. New York: Macmillan, 1970 [1969].

Spinoza, Benedict de. *Ethics*. In *The Chief Works of Benedict de Spinoza*, translated by R. H. M. Elwes, 2:43–271. New York: Dover, 1955 [1677].

Ssu-ma Ch'ien. *The Grand Scribe's Records*. Translated by Weiguo Cao, Scott W. Galer, William H. Nienhauser, Jr., and David W. Pankenicr. 7 vols. Bloomington: Indiana University Press, 1994–2002 [1st century BC].

Stengel, Richard. *(You're Too Kind): A Brief History of Flattery*. New York: Simon & Schuster, 2000.

Stewarton [Lewis Goldsmith]. *Secret Memoirs of the Court of St. Cloud, in a Series of Letters from a Gentleman at Paris to a Nobleman in London*. 2 vols. Boston: Grolier Society, 1905.

Suetonius, Gaius. *Lives of the Caesars*. Translated by J. C. Rolfe. 2 vols. Cambridge: Harvard University Press [c. AD 120].

Surtees, Robert Smith. *The Analysis of the Hunting Field*. New York: Charles Scribner's Sons, 1931 [1846].

Tacitus. *Agricola, Germanicus, Dialogus*. Translated by M. Hutton and W. Peterson, revised by R. M. Ovilgie, E. H. Warmington, and M. Winterbottom. Cambridge: Harvard University Press, 1985.

———. *Annals*. Translated by John Jackson. 3 vols. Cambridge: Harvard University Press, 1969 [AD 116].

———. *The Histories*. Translated by C. H. Moore. 2 vols. Cambridge: Harvard University Press, 1985 [c. AD 100–110].

Taine, Hippolyte Adolphe. *The French Revolution*. Translated by John Durand. 3 vols. New York: Henry Holt, 1878–85 [1876–81].

Talleyrand, Charles Maurice de, Prince de. *Memoirs*. Edited by the duc de Broglie. Translated by Mrs. Agnus Hall. 5 vols. New York: G. P. Putnam's Sons, 1892.

Tertullian. "The Apology." Translated by Rev. S. Thelwall. In *The Ante-*

Nicene Fathers, vol. 3, *Latin Christianity: Its Founder, Tertullian*, edited by Alexander Roberts and James Donaldson, 17–60. New York: Christian Literature, 1890 [c. AD 200].

———. "On Modesty." Translated by A. Cleveland Coxe. In *The Ante-Nicene Fathers*, edited by Alexander Roberts and James Donaldson, 4:74–101. New York: Christian Literature, 1885 [c. AD 200].

Theophilus. *Theophilus to Autolycus*. Translated by Rev. Marcus Dods. In *The Ante-Nicene Fathers*, vol. 2, *Fathers of the Second Century*, edited by Alexander Roberts and James Donaldson, 89–122. New York: Christian Literature, 1890 [mid-2nd century AD].

Theophrastus. *The Characters*. Translated by Philip Vellacott. Harmondsworth: Penguin, 1967 [3rd century BC].

Thomas à Kempis. *The Christian's Pattern; or, The Imitation of Jesus Christ*. London: W. Reeve, 1753 [c. 1450].

Thoreau, Henry David. *Walden and Civil Disobedience*. Edited by Owen Thomas. New York: W. W. Norton, 1981 [1854].

Tocqueville, Alexis de. *Democracy in America*. Translated by Harvey C. Mansfield and Delba Winthrop. Chicago: University of Chicago Press, 2000 [1835, 1840].

Tolstoy, L. N. *Resurrection*. Translated by Rosemary Edmonds. Harmondsworth: Penguin, 1966 [1889–1900].

———. *War and Peace*. Translated by Constance Garnett. New York: Random House, 1950 [1865–69].

The Tso chuan. Translated by Burton Watson. New York: Columbia University Press, 1989 [c. 490 BC].

Varty, Kenneth. *Reynard, Renart, Reinaert, and Other Foxes in Medieval England: The Iconographic Evidence*. Amsterdam: Amsterdam University Press, 1999.

Vermes, Geza. *The Complete Dead Sea Scrolls in English*. New York: Allen Lane Penguin, 1997.

Walsingham, Edward. *Manual of Prudential Maxims for Statesmen and Courtiers*. See Raleigh.

Walters, Kerry S. *Benjamin Franklin and His Gods*. Champaign: University of Illinois Press, 1999.

Washington, George. *Writings*. Edited by John Rhodehamel. New York: Library of America, 1997.

White, Andrew Dickson. *History of the Warfare of Science with Theology in Christendom*. New York: George Braziller, 1955 [1896].

Woodville, William. *Medical Botany: Containing Systematic and General Descriptions.* 4 vols. London: James Philips, 1790–93.

Wright, George. *The Gentleman's Miscellany.* Exeter: H. Ranlet, 1797.

Yogananda, Paramahansa. *Autobiography of a Yogi.* Los Angeles: Self-Realization Fellowship, 1981 [1946].

INDEX

In the *Stages* Series

21. "All hail the victor!" Reynard triumphant, by Walter von Kaulbach (1846).